MICHAEL REDGRAVE
My Father

MICHAEL REDGRAVE
My Father

by

CORIN REDGRAVE

RICHARD COHEN BOOKS • London

British Library Cataloguing in Publication Data:
A catalogue record for this book is available from the British Library

Copyright © 1995 by Corin Redgrave

ISBN 1 86066 000 2

First published in Great Britain in 1995 by
Richard Cohen Books
7 Manchester Square,
London WIM 5RE

1 3 5 7 9 8 6 4 2

Typeset in Linotron 202 Sabon by
Rowland Phototypesetting Ltd,
Bury St Edmunds, Suffolk

Printed in Great Britain by
Mackays of Chatham plc

To Luke

When I read the book, the biography famous,
And is this then (I said) what the author calls a man's life?

And so will some one when I am dead and gone write of my life?
(As if any man really knew aught of my life,
Why even I myself I often think know little or nothing of my real life,

Only a few hints, a few diffused faint clews and indirections
I seek for my own use to trace out here.)

Walt Whitman, 'Leaves of Grass', 1871

Contents

List of Illustrations

✿

MR as Laertes and Laurence Olivier as Hamlet in *Hamlet*, the Old Vic, 1937 (Angus McBean, Mander & Mitchenson)

MR with Margaret Lockwood, Dame May Whitty and Basil Radford in *The Lady Vanishes*, 1938 (Kobal Collection)

MR and Diana Wynyard in *Kipps*, 1941 (Kobal Collection)

MR and Bob Michell in Hollywood, 1947

Bob Michell

MR in bathing suit, 1930s

Between pages 146–147

News Chronicle headline, 4 March 1941

MR in the Royal Navy, front row, centre, 1941

MR and Vanessa at Bedford House, late 1940s, author sitting on steps (Howard Byrne, Piccadilly Press)

MR and Lynn, 1940s

MR with the author, 1940s (Pictorial Press)

The family at Bedford House, 1946 (Pictorial Press)

MR as Macbeth, Aldwych Theatre, 1947

Bryan Kneale's portrait of MR as Hamlet, Stratford-upon-Avon, 1958 (from the RSC Collection, with the permission of the Governors of the Royal Shakespeare Company)

MR as Antony and Peggy Ashcroft as Cleopatra in *Antony and Cleopatra*, in rehearsal at the Prince's Theatre, 1953 (Hulton Deutsch)

MR, Nancy Coleman, Kirk Douglas and Katina Paxinou in *Mourning Becomes Electra*, for which MR received an Oscar nomination, 1951

MR with Brian Smith in *The Browning Version*, 1950, for which he won the prize for best actor at the Cannes Film Festival, the first English actor to do so

MR as King Lear, Stratford-upon-Avon, 1953

MR as Hamlet, Stratford-upon-Avon, 1958 (from the RSC Collection, with the permission of the Governors of the Royal Shakespeare Company)

MR at Angkor Thom, Cambodia, a break from shooting *The Quiet American* in Saigon, 1957 (Raymond Voinquel)

Moscow tour, 1958–9. Angela Baddeley, MR, Dorothy Tutin, tour guide, Coral Browne, Rachel Kempson and Geraldine McEwan (Hulton Deutsch)

MR and Vanessa

MR and the author (Kika Markham)

The family at MR's funeral, March 1985 (Newsline)

As King Lear, with Vanessa, at the Roundhouse in London, 1982 (Newsline)

Acknowledgements

The author and publishers gratefully acknowledge the following for permission to reproduce copyright material:

The Eliot estate, Faber & Faber Ltd amd Harcourt Brace & Company for the lines from *The Family Reunion* by T. S. Eliot; Faber & Faber Ltd and Random House Inc for the lines from 'August for the People and their Favourite Islands' in *The English Auden: Poems, Essays and Dramatic Writings 1927–1939* by W. H. Auden, edited by Edward Mendelson; A. M. Heath & Co Ltd and Harcourt Brace Jovanovich Inc for the extract from George Orwell's 'Wartime Diary', from *The Collected Essays, Journalism and Letters*, copyright © George Orwell; Weidenfeld & Nicolson and Viking for extracts from *In My Mind's Eye* by Michael Redgrave.

I

Overture and Finale

⚥

Looking back, the whole thing seems faintly ludicrous, as quarrels in the family do when seen from a safe distance. But at the time it was painful enough.

'I quite understand', wrote my younger sister, 'that you would like to bury Dad's ashes near Karl Marx. I should have preferred St Paul's, the actors' church in Covent Garden, and so would Mum I think. But your choice means more to you than ours would to us, so you should go ahead.'

Which was generous, indeed – though in fact my choice of Highgate Cemetery had almost nothing to do with Karl Marx. His great, grey tomb lies on the eastern side of Swains Lane, the side which is open to the public, large enough to defy any but the most desperate attempt at desecration, but too slab and forbidding for the man whose work it commemorates.

My small plot of earth lies on the west side. Iron gates span the arch of the gatehouse. Beyond is a handsome gravelled courtyard backed by a long curved wall with blind arches, and in the centre of the wall a flight of steps mounts upward.

Twice a day guided tours visit the graves of the famous and the forgotten. At other times the west side is closed to the public. Here cowslips grow in the long grass, and squirrels and badgers play among the gravestones: a very fine and private place, planted, tended and sprinkled with the annual subscriptions of the 'Friends of Highgate Cemetery'. Apart from these, and the entrance fees they charge to visitors on the east side,

Highgate relies for its income on covenants, donations, and the sale of burial or cremation plots.

I paid £600 for my father's plot, about four feet long by two and a half feet wide, too small by half for a grave, but giving ample space for all that remains after a cremation. Freehold, of course. £600, though more than I could well afford at the time, had bought a patch of eternity.

But, having bought my plot of earth, I had nothing left to buy a headstone, not even in Cumberland slate. And then I should have to find the price of the engraving, at so much a letter. My fortunes were at a low ebb. And yet it never occurred to me to borrow the money, or ask the other members of my family to share the cost. His ashes would simply have to wait a little longer before I could bury them.

In the meantime I could still go to Highgate, and in fine weather sit on my plot of grass and ponder on a possible inscription. I don't think it occurred to me during those months of gentle, selfish dreaming that though I alone might have bought his grave he was not my father only, nor should I only decide matters which others might have an interest in.

Then a letter arrived from New York, from my younger sister.

Saturday 21 August 1993

Dear Corin

Hope you are all well – and have had a wonderful holiday.

I was extremely upset to get a call from the *Evening Standard* who had been sleuthing the fate of Dad's Ashes. The guy said he was about to call Mother and that he had her number. I called her to warn her to try to avoid her saying anything that could be quoted.

Anyway, it is now over a year since our correspondence re the best place to finally bury Dad's ashes. (I checked my Diary, it was while I was in London 12–22 May 1992.)

Eight years and six months since Dad's death. And *still* his ashes sit in Mortlake.

I enclose a copy of Mum's letter to me. She has *always* wanted them to be at St Paul's Covent Garden and as you will see has been led to believe that they are indeed there and that makes her happy.

So, I have made a call to Mortlake who say that only your signature can release the ashes, since you were the one who arranged the cremation.

I have asked them to send you a form to sign that will allow me or another family member or representative to collect the ashes and take them to St Paul's as per Mum's wishes.

Corin, this is a matter that is deeply upsetting to me and has been the cause of anxiety to Mother (and I don't mean the *Evening Standard* only. I mean that the ashes are still at Mortlake.). So please I beg of you – allow us all to put this matter (and Dad) to rest.

Kelly will be in UK in the next few weeks and could take care of this.

With love Lynny

PS Please let me hear from you.

Clipped to Lynn's letter was a copy of the article from the *Evening Standard* 'Londoner's Diary'. I noticed it had appeared on 5 August, while I was away with my children in France. It was the first item in the 'Diary', under the headline 'Redgrave's Ashes on the Shelf'.

There are those who wish their ashes to be scattered at sea or over a favourite pasture with a fond remembrance. But there are surely few people who would like them to have been sitting unmourned and unloved on a shelf in the Mortlake Crematorium for the last eight years.

Such, however, is the fate of the last remains of Sir Michael Redgrave, one of our finest post-war actors and father to an entire brood of thespians. He died aged 77 in 1985, since when his ashes have rented space at Mortlake for £2 a month.

'Quite a lot of urns are left here, but Sir Michael is the only famous person we have,' a Mortlake assistant, Mrs Spoke, tells me. 'We keep them in a room downstairs.'

That there has been no burial or recognition does not seem to concern Redgrave's nearest and dearest, his widow Rachel and children Vanessa, Lynn and Corin.

'I thought somebody would have collected them by now,' Lynn Redgrave tells me nonchalantly. She is currently appearing in *Shakespeare for My Father* in New York. 'I left it to other members of the family to decide where his last resting place should be.'

Then follows a very perplexing paragraph:

It is perhaps not surprising that the family has behaved in this way. In his autobiography, *In My Mind's Eye*, Redgrave revealed he did not have the will power to 'starve off the other side of my nature'.

The reference to my father's autobiography was odd. The journalist had misquoted the text. What Michael actually wrote was 'I cannot feel it would be right – even if I had the will-power, which I have not – to cut off or starve the other side of my nature.' My father was bisexual. He wanted to write about it but never managed to, and this delicate and rather ambiguous hint is the only mention he makes of it in his autobiography. Picked up and quoted out of context, as here in the 'Londoner's Diary', it loses its delicacy, becoming instead a mere nod and a wink to the knowing reader, as if the diarist, even in these outspoken times, only permitted himself this rather oblique 'outing' of a bisexual.

And what on earth did the writer have in mind when he said it was 'perhaps not surprising that the family has behaved in this way'? Did he imagine we were embarrassed by Michael's affairs, and thought that the best way of hiding them would be to let his ashes lie out of sight? Or was he suggesting that bisexual people are not only promiscuous but disloyal, and that their children must inherit their disloyalty?

What was even stranger was that the journalist ended his piece with a very positive proposal as to the proper place for Michael's ashes.

The most obvious resting place for his ashes is the actors' church, St Paul's, Covent Garden, an idea that is greeted with enthusiasm by the rector, David Elliott. 'We wouldn't actually store the ashes, but they could be buried in the churchyard. If the family approached us we'd almost certainly say yes to that.'

I had the uncomfortable feeling that I was being tricked. What could have prompted the *Evening Standard*, after all these years, to investigate the fate of my father's ashes? As hard as I tried I could not banish the idea that my sister had planted the story. But why? Publicity? Her play was doing very well on Broadway. Why should she want publicity of this kind in London? I felt ashamed of myself for even asking such a question, and tried hard to put it out of mind. I was well on the way to succeeding when a long review of Lynn's play appeared in the London *Times* a few days later. 'An ogre of a parent if ever there was one,' wrote Peter Pringle, describing the impression he had of Michael's cavalier attitude to parenting, 'witness the extraordinary revelation last week that his ashes are still sitting in an urn in Mortlake Crematorium, unclaimed by any of the surviving family: Lynn, sister Vanessa, brother Corin and Sir Michael's widow, Rachel.'

In this version, our neglect of a burial for Michael's ashes had become a calculated negligence, our collective rejection as children of our 'ogre' of a parent. I began to feel a prickling sensation of guilt, and cast around for someone to blame. Again I became firmly convinced that all Lynn's commotion over Michael's ashes was an exercise in advance publicity, preparing the way for her play to transfer to a West End theatre. Buzzing with anger I sat down to write a sarcastic letter to New York, but was stopped in my tracks by the arrival of a third letter, from the director of Mortlake Crematorium, a Mr R. A. Coates. 'I do apologise', he wrote, 'for the distress that article must have caused you. Our staff have strict instructions not to speak to the Press, but I'm afraid the instructions were ignored on this occasion.'

So that was it. Mrs Spoke, 'a Mortlake assistant' as the 'Londoner's Diary' described her, had spoken. I might have given her a piece of my mind, but by now the anger was abating. And in any case what proof had I that the *Standard* had not telephoned, asking for confirmation that Michael's ashes were there, and that she, poor innocent Mrs Spoke, naïve as to the ways of the press, had not simply answered, yes, they were?

After all, I realised, I must stop searching for someone else to blame for my distress and face up to the fact that I had brought it on myself. When all was said and done, Michael had died on 21 March 1985. I was there at his bedside, I had arranged his cremation a few days later, and now it was August 1993, and his ashes were still at Mortlake.

I rang the crematorium to say I was coming down and would collect my father's ashes. They turned out to be not in an urn but in a small wooden box. I put it on the back seat of my car and drove home.

Next day I wrote to Lynn. I told her I had collected the ashes and would keep them safely until she, Vanessa, Rachel and I could meet and decide what to do with them. That night I gave a lift to a friend, and noticed as he was about to sit in the front seat that the box of ashes was still on the back seat. I put it in the boot.

And there they remained for several weeks. Strange as it might seem, I felt comforted by them. After a while I began to wonder how I had ever managed without them. Alone in my car, driving down Trinity Road, the long straight road that goes from Balham to the Thames, I would play music to them, and even sing to them. Sometimes they would sing back, a distant, clear, pure baritone – 'every valley shall be exalted'. Once, when Radio 3 was playing Haydn's 'Miracle' symphony, I could hear them laughing.

It couldn't last, and of course it didn't. My mother decided she was going to New York to see Lynn's play, 'and of course I must take Michael's ashes to St Paul's, I've promised Lynn I would.'

For one brief second of a flicker of resistance I thought of taking Michael's ashes from their box and of substituting some ashes from my grate. Who could possibly tell the difference? I hated the thought of Michael's ashes cold in the earth of Covent Garden.

But when the day came my mother seemed happy to see them buried there, and the churchwarden promised to plant a rose.

2

The Biography of an Autobiography

☙

On board the aircraft carrier HMS *Enterprise* as an ordinary seaman in the navy my father kept himself awake during the long hours of the night watch by torturing his memory to recall every detail of the furnishings of his stepfather's dining-room at 9 Chapel Street, Belgravia. Some time nearer the end of the war the publisher Collins invited him to write his life story. He liked to refer to this as an 'agreement'. It was never so definite as a commission or a contract, and he obviously wanted it that way because a contract would have tied him to a timetable, whereas he preferred to tease himself with the infinitely post-ponable pain and pleasure of writing his memoirs.

It was not that he found the act of writing difficult. From his schooldays at Clifton College he was a conscientious diarist, only occasionally lapsing into silence, filling numerous note-books and yearbooks until 1969 when for some reason he stopped writing. After the first self-conscious flourishes – 'God speed, little diary!' – his voice settles down, becoming terse and nervy, like his own inner voice.

Three plays, two books about acting and a novel, *The Moun-tebank's Tale*, testify to his skill as a writer. All were published, and one of them, *An Actor's Ways and Means*, has lately been republished, more than forty years after the text was first heard as four Rockefeller Lectures at Bristol University. But some-where on the way to his autobiography he wrote two chapters about his childhood, and they are so fluent, witty and assured that he must have felt confident that the whole story, when it came, would come naturally.

I do not know exactly when these chapters were written, but I feel sure it was several years before he began to write the whole book. Their success does not seem to have prompted him to get on with the job: quite the contrary. If I have guessed their date correctly, about 1952, they seem to have convinced him that he could afford to take his time – which is unfortunate, because nothing quite as good, nothing as elegant, was achieved by more than a quarter of a century's postponing.

The first chapter unfolds a sentence of prodigious length, the fruit of those long night watches in the Atlantic, as he describes the terrifying dining-room in his stepfather's house. The technique owes something to the resources of cinema. His sentence unwinds at the same steady pace as a camera would pan round a room, and the tone of his voice is as even as off-screen narration.

It was after breakfast, and Aunt Mabel and I were alone in the dining-room of my stepfather's house off Belgrave Square. She had been telling me stories about Roy, my father, whom I did not remember, and of whom I knew next to nothing, and little good . . .

As I recall it I can almost taste the Ceylon 'Breakfast' tea, see again the gloomy light of that dining-room, with its dark red damask curtains, its embossed wallpaper looking like crocodile skin, the Persian carpets, the electrified alabaster bowl which hung above the oddly square dining-table and cast such a waxy light on the faces of the diners, the rows of books bought by the yard, Dickens and Scott in Library Editions, *The Beaux and Belles of England* in half-leather bindings which all too neatly filled the glazed upper parts of the huge three-piece secretaire whose lower parts housed the best tea service and the cut-glass tumblers and wineglasses, the large, handsome sideboards, the heavy decanters of whisky and port, the epergne shaped like a cluster of tall tropical trees with a cut-glass fruit bowl resting in their delicate silver branches and a Singalese shepherd reclining in their shade (a gift to my stepfather from the Ceylon and Eastern Agency when he retired). All these, I feel, as I remember Aunt Mabel that day, might still be there, if only I did not know for certain that they are not. Still there, still kept in spotless order by Mary, the parlour maid from County Wicklow, mute witnesses of dining-room conversations that were usually strained, because nothing unpleasant, no discomfortable fact, must ever be mentioned, and long silences, even at breakfast, were not allowed. It was the one room in the house which I really hated; it was so hard to escape from it.

'Discomfortable', meaning 'causing discomfort', is an obsolete word, and has been for a while. Shakespeare's Richard II uses it, in that great speech to his cousin Aumerle about the divine right of kings, after he returns from Ireland:

> Discomfortable cousin! know'st thou not
> That when the searching eye of heaven is hid . . .
> Then thieves and robbers range abroad unseen
> In murthers and in outrage boldly here.

Michael played Richard in the cycle of history plays at Stratford in 1951. Probably the first chapter of his autobiography was written not long after, while Richard's vocabulary was still fresh in his memory.

The second chapter describes a holiday *en famille* on the coast of Normandy.

If I set aside my early trip to Australia and back, I suppose my first foreign holiday occurred when I was about sixteen, when Mother, Andy, Peggy, and I went to Normandy, to the small, delightfully-named watering-place Veules-les-Roses, where we stayed at the important-sounding Hôtel des Bains et de la Plage, a small, second-rate hotel near the sea. The bathing was poor, off a shingle beach, backed by chalk cliffs. The hotel food was sometimes suspected of being of equine origin, dressed up with watercress.

But it was 'abroad'. There were charming, poppy-sprinkled walks through the fields at the top of the cliffs. There was a 'casino': a rather shabby affair where one could dance to a trio, and an inner room where the grown-ups could gamble for small stakes. 'Yes, We Have No Bananas' was the rage of Veules that year and I danced to it evening after evening with a beautiful, tall, dark American girl with the Shakespearian name of Mary Arden Stead.

The year after my father's death in 1985 I was driving with my wife Kika Markham and our two small boys towards Dieppe, at the end of our holiday in France. Suddenly, without sign or warning, we came upon Veules-les-Roses. With a lump in my throat I saw how little had changed since Michael had stayed there. The Hôtel des Bains had recently been converted into private apartments, but the casino was still there. The Normandy coast is like that. Nothing changes, and except for the occasional intrusion of high spirits or violence it remains becalmed in mild-mannered gentility which bears less and less relation to the country inland.

Between the two beautifully written chapters and the book in which they eventually appeared as the first and fourth chapter respectively, more than a quarter of a century passed before 'the agreement' was finally acted upon.

It was 1981, and the publishers were Viking and Weidenfeld; by this time Collins had dropped out. Since my father had acquired a literary agent, what in the glory of his heyday as a film star and leading actor had been sufficient as a gentleman's agreement had now become a contract. Fortunately it was quite a lucrative contract, because by now he was crippled with Parkinson's disease and unable to work as an actor. In fact he was almost unable to write. Tablets of Sinemet, a preparation containing L-dopa, controlled his tremors sufficiently for him to hold a pen and guide it across the page, but his strength was wasted and the pen moved so slowly and awkwardly that his writing, after shaping one or two words well enough, staggered drunkenly up and down from the horizontal. That was how I came to be enrolled as his helper. I was working in Yorkshire at the time. But for three days every week I would travel to Wilks Water, my mother's cottage in Hampshire, and sit with him in his garden studio, notebook and tape recorder beside me.

I knew it would not be easy. I realised there must be episodes in his life that he would feel more hesitant to talk about with me than he might have with a professional secretary. I knew I would have to sit patiently, enduring long periods of silence, punctuated by my short questions and his monosyllabic replies. Michael was an excellent raconteur but a hopeless conversationalist. Given the right setting, and an audience he liked and trusted, he could entertain effortlessly. In conversation, though, his responses would freeze. He would seek any excuse and retire to his bedroom, or confront his questioners with a painful blank stare focused three or four inches above their heads.

'Be careful, the wind might change, and that look will stay on your face for ever,' people used to say to children. In Michael's case the wind changed cruelly, and the blank stare which I feared as a child became in illness his permanent expression. Parkinson's disease seems to find sadistic pleasure in robbing people of their most precious attributes. It robbed Mohammed Ali, the 'greatest', of his quicksilver movements and slowed him to a shuffle, and it robbed my father of his power, especially remarkable in films, to show in his face every nuance of his feeling. 'The mask' as it is known in medical literature, because it conceals all expression, descended upon his face. Only his eyes spoke for him through the mask, questioning, imploring, seeking contact. His voice sounded throttled and distant.

He was using the garden studio as a refuge, but he no longer slept there. To reach the main cottage from the studio you had to cross a bridge made of wooden planks over a little stream. In summer the stream was a mere trickle, but in winter it was a babbling torrent, and one night in the winter of 1980–1 Michael wandered off the bridge on the way to the cottage and ended up face down in the icy water. Goodness knows what prompted my mother to go out and find him there. His cries, if he made them, could not have been louder than the noise of the water. And heaven knows where she found the strength to raise him from the stream. At thirteen and a half stone he was heavy enough to raise to his feet even when fully conscious and co-operative. Waterlogged and half conscious, he must have been harder to raise than Lazarus. But raise him she did. There is something truly Homeric about my mother.

Now therefore he slept in the main cottage. But he still used the studio as a retreat, and it was there that we retired after lunch on the first day of his autobiography. Michael settled himself comfortably in his chair and fell asleep. An hour later he was still asleep and by then my eyelids were flickering. It was a warm summer afternoon. Butterflies fluttered in the lavender bush outside the studio door and a gentle breeze stirred in the leaves of the catalpa tree. I fell asleep myself. An hour later I woke and looked at my father, still asleep, though in an instant his eyes also opened and he said, 'You seem to be rather tired.'

Three days passed in this way, and I returned to Doncaster without a word written. Realising a change of tactic was called for, I telephoned to suggest that the following week we should meet in the morning. I prepared a series of questions, hoping they would stir something. They didn't. He fended them all off with the most cursory replies, as if I were an incompetent, troublesome interviewer. Eventually, in desperation, I did begin to sound, even to my own ears, like the juvenile scribbler on a provincial newspaper he seemed to think I was.

'What about your Hamlet?' I asked, apropos of nothing. There was nothing to be apropos of. He was destroying all connections.

'What about it?' he replied.

'Tell us about it.'

'Oh no, I've said all there is to say about it. I don't want to say it again, for heaven's sake.'

'But Dad,' I protested, 'whatever you may have said in the past has been remembered or forgotten by those who read it. Now you're writing your autobiography for a generation which never read anything you said but are interested to hear what you have to say now.'

'Why should they be?'

We were getting nowhere. The second week passed as fruitlessly as the first. When the third week came I decided upon a desperate gambit. While Michael slept I wrote a whole chapter about his schooldays. I thought it was quite a successful pastiche. I had read everything he'd written. I knew his life, so I thought, as well if not better than he knew it himself. I could imitate not only his tone of voice but his vocabulary and patterns of speech. When he awoke, on the third day, I read it over to him.

'What do you think?'

'It's very good. There's only one problem.'

'What's that?'

'I didn't write it myself.'

'I know that,' I said, hardly able to contain my sarcasm. 'You haven't written anything or dictated anything for two weeks.'

Parkinson's disease can be long drawn out, painful and wearisome. In its later stages a patient's motor control is so depleted that even to advance one foot in front of the other requires an exhausting effort. But put an obstacle in front of his foot and he will step over it without hesitation. I found this useful hint in a little booklet published by the Parkinson's Society. And so it proved with my father. And so indeed it proved in this case. My presumption in writing a passage for him released what had been locked up and he began to dictate. Slowly, but with flawless syntax, he dictated what would become the second chapter.

Some autobiographers load the first part of their book with a great deal of ballast concerning grandfathers, great-grandfathers, uncles and aunts, and the reader must endure all this solemn parade of ancestors to earn the privilege of being introduced to the author in his pram. Not so my father, who had no ancestors to speak of, being the illegitimate son of two actors, George Ellsworthy 'Roy' Redgrave and Daisy Scudamore. Roy was a barnstorming actor who emigrated to Australia the year after Michael was born. Michael's early childhood, after his mother Daisy gave up the pursuit of Roy in Australia, was a fabulous world of digs and dressing-rooms, and late-night meals at whelk stalls in the Mile End Road.

My father re-created this world from memory easily and with touching affection. Dictation, once he had begun, hardly taxed him at all. He could invent pages of dialogue without blushing. My part, so far, was simply to write down his dictation in longhand, since I had found early on that the tape recorder inhibited him. Once or twice, more for amusement than relief, we would drive to one of the scenes of his childhood, Battersea Bridge Road, or Faunce Street in Kennington where he shared a bed with Daisy, and where Florrie the housemaid would run upstairs to the lodgers, mostly actors, with trays of breakfast.

I realised, having read his diaries, that his memory cast a warm glow of affection on many of the cast of characters from his childhood and youth. His stepfather J. P. Anderson was the chief beneficiary. None the less his introduction of this character is beautifully contrived. He is first glimpsed as a mysterious gentleman caller, dressed in the uniform of an army captain, tiptoeing from Michael's mother's digs in the early hours of the morning. This is seen through the anxious, jealous eyes of a five-year-old boy who is deeply in love with his mother.

Then one day when the boy is playing in the backyard of his lodgings in Cricklewood, where for a month or more he has been exiled and separated from his mother, a chauffeur-driven car arrives and he is told to pack up his belongings immediately. What is more strange, the dull and stupid little girl called Peg, who has been his companion in these lodgings for the past month or so, is to come with him. They are driven to a street in Belgravia, where a maid in a mob-cap curtsies on the doorstep, and where in the hall his mother is waiting to show him his new home. Upstairs a bedroom has been decorated just for him. And next door, decorated in pink, is a bedroom for little Peg. 'Is she staying with us?' he asks. His mother looks at him very seriously and tells him he now has a sister. Then she holds him very close – an unusual gesture, this, because she hardly ever held him close – and tells him to go downstairs to the drawing-room, knock on the door, and go up to a man whose name is Andy. This man, Michael realises, is the mysterious gentleman caller. 'You must sit on his knee, and give him a kiss, and call him Daddy.'

After this introduction 'Andy' – as J. P. Anderson is always referred to – becomes a gruff, genial Scot whose generosity to his stepson is dutifully recorded at every stage. I knew from my father's diaries that his stepfather's mere proximity could inspire in Michael a searing, scornful rage. But his recollection seventy years later airbrushes almost every trace of contempt and hatred from the picture.

His mother fares similarly. In fact I have to curb myself from seeing Daisy as the main cause of Michael's worst problems. She was an actress who had graduated too suddenly from playing the soubrette in light comedy and the heroine in melodrama and Grand Guignol to the dignified matriarchal roles in Shaw, Galsworthy and J. M. Barrie that were more suited to her new role in life as the wife of a wealthy retired tea-planter. She became a secret drinker, and finally a dipsomaniac, and could never reconcile herself to her son's prodigious talent, blaming him always for the boredom, the respectable living death, of her second marriage to Andy. Her letters to Michael, and especially her letters to her sister Mabel, harp endlessly on Michael's alleged ingratitude. In fact all his life seems to me a baffled unsuccessful attempt to earn her gratitude and praise. But again little or none of this surfaces in his autobiography.

At seventy-four he loved to dwell on his childhood. In fact almost any part of his life amused him except his life as an actor. I had to coax his performances from him syllable by syllable. The only exception was those performances about which he could indulge in a peculiarly English, half-tragic, half-comic self-deprecation. In these cases his fancy soared, and he could freely invent pages of dialogue. The best of these descriptions finds him, together with his leading lady Sylvia Coleridge, on their hands and knees searching for pieces of a radio receiver. It was the first night of a new play by William Trevor, *The Old Boys*, in 1971. Michael was suffering from Parkinson's disease, though it was still undiagnosed, and was unable to learn his lines. So the stage manager prompted him, line by line, and he picked up each prompt, one line at a time, through an ear-piece attached to a radio in his jacket pocket – or, rather, that was what was meant to happen. In fact on the first night he panicked, and turned down the volume when he should have turned it up, fiddled with his ear-piece, dropped it, then dropped the receiver, which smashed into a thousand pieces on the stage of the Mermaid Theatre.

The only other subject he would not or could not write about was the nature of his sexuality. During one of our early sessions in his garden studio I suggested to him that he might wish to 'come out' and write about his bisexuality. I'm sure I never used that phrase, and probably didn't even know it at the time. But I know that my suggestion, however clumsy and formal it must have sounded, was unambiguous. Michael's reply was equally unequivocal. 'I shall certainly write about that,' he said. But months passed and he never broached the subject.

Then one afternoon the subject broached itself. I had promised to stay with my father for a week instead of the usual three days, but for some reason I had to return to Yorkshire well before our week was up. When I told him that we should have to leave together the following day he stubbornly refused. As my mother was filming abroad, I insisted that Michael must come with me. It was quite impossible for him to remain on his own. The cottage was at least a mile from the nearest habitation, and there was no one to help him if he should get into difficulties. 'Someone is coming,' he replied mysteriously. When I asked him, unbelievingly, who this visitor might be, he shouted, as if all the force of his lungs had returned, 'My friend!'

Mischievously I asked, 'What friend?' Well, not entirely mischievously, perhaps. Who could believe that my father, with his shakes and tremors, could still . . . ?

'My lover!' he bellowed.

'Oh, I see.'

I felt chastened, shaken. I knew he had a friend whose name was Alan. My mother had met Alan twice, very briefly, and had formed the impression that he was about twenty years younger than my father, with a South London accent, a cab-driver perhaps, or a doorman at a hotel. But I had never met the man and I guessed my father felt a little ashamed of his relationship, as if he were exploiting Alan, or perhaps as if Alan were exploiting him. In any case I doubted if Alan would be likely to want half a week in a wood in Hampshire, where the nearest pub was a two-mile walk away, tending my invalid father.

I telephoned my elder sister and persuaded her to catch the next train to Winchfield. Half an hour later I shouted up to my father that I was leaving.

'All right,' he called out feebly.

'Vanessa will be here in an hour,' I shouted back.

I paused for his reply, but there was none. As I drove down the lane I bit my lip in disgust at the maladroit way I had behaved. Surely I should have gone upstairs and explained why I had telephoned for Vanessa? Would he not think either that I had called her to spoil the few days he had wanted alone with Alan, or, worse, that I had doubted whether Alan would come at all?

The following week I tried once more to broach the forbidden subject. We were nearing the end of the book, and the sense of relief at having almost completed our journey was palpable.

'Why don't you write about Alan?' I asked.

'He wouldn't want me to.'

What more could I say? But Michael clearly felt there should have been more, or at least that he owed me some more explanation, because many hours later, as if unconscious of the lapse of time, he remarked suddenly:

'I think they saw us together.'

He had spent the night with Alan in my mother's mews cottage in London. The next morning as Alan was leaving he had kissed him goodbye. The door was half open and the titled lady who lived opposite had walked past and seen them kissing. She was distantly related to the immensely wealthy family which owned the mews and many acres in Belgravia.

'Why worry?' I said. 'She's probably seen as much, or more, a few times in her life. She might be quite broad-minded.'

'Oh, you don't know,' my father said, and shuddered as if pinched by a cold draught.

3

On the Way Out

℧

Not since I was a child and prayed fervently for my father's success did I wish him success so much as for *In My Mind's Eye* when it was published in 1983. I wanted it to redeem the neglect he suffered from since he had been forced to quit the stage, and if I am honest I think I wanted it also for myself. I had quit the stage too, though voluntarily. Working with him for three days a week had been my parole, when I could revisit vicariously the paradise my chosen life in politics had excluded me from. In Yorkshire, where I spent the remainder of each week, I was an organiser for the Workers' Revolutionary Party.

There is something of me in *In My Mind's Eye*. As time went on and my father grew more tired, whole chapters fell to me to complete and sometimes even write entirely; but I invented almost nothing that had not been said in some other form, such as letters, diaries, essays or postcards. The only thing I invented was the sound of his voice. Of course this does not detract from his achievement.

One of the publicity events organised by Alex McCormack, Michael's editor, was at the National Film Theatre, where Adrian Lyon edited together a special film in tribute to Michael, with excerpts from some of his best performances in the cinema. It began with his opening scene as Gilbert in Hitch-cock's 1938 film *The Lady Vanishes*. I introduced it by reading a passage from his book in which he remembers feeling pretty contemptuous of the business of filming. He was playing every night in John Gielgud's famous company at the Queen's Theatre, and compared with his evenings in Shaftesbury Avenue filming in Islington seemed laboured and thoroughly artificial. As for the script, he thought it insufferably callow. Some of this shows in that first scene where Gilbert bursts uninvited into Margaret Lockwood's bedroom. But what predominates in his playing is a careless unselfconsciousness which exactly complements Hitchcock's cynical attitude to the art he so completely mastered.

Soon afterwards we went to the Dorchester for Christina Foyle's literary luncheon. Great pains had been taken to assemble a gathering worthy of the occasion. Alec Guinness was there. Michael always deferred to Guinness, thinking, like Garrick, that 'you can fool the town in tragedy, but comedy will find you out.' John Clements was there, the best Henry Higgins I ever saw and the only one, not excluding Rex Harrison's, who could refer to 'my Miltonic mind' without risk of embarrassing his audience. John Mills was there, looking uncannily like himself. Lord Gowrie delivered the eulogy, relaxed, urbane and yet modest, full of thumbnail portraits of Michael's performances so deft that one really believed the speaker had seen them.

Then it was Michael's turn. Of course he was not obliged to speak and it was certainly not expected of him. But he felt as keenly as ever the actor's hunger for surprise, for astonishment, for Diaghilev's 'Jean, étonne-moi!' Accordingly he had come prepared, though not even Alex McCormack was allowed to share the secret. All enquiries had been fended off with disarming modesty – 'Nothing much, but you may rather enjoy it.' Word had got around, and a satisfyingly large army of photographers was on hand to greet his arrival at the Dorchester with my mother.

To me only he had confided that he was not going to make a speech but would recite a cockney music-hall monologue which had been his party piece for the last sixty years. It began life with Little Tich and probably ended with Michael. It was something to do with a lady being hauled down Worthing beach in a bathing machine, shyly stepping into the briny and being knocked over by a wave, to the amusement of the onlookers. The whole thing was recited very fast in a breathy rasping monotone and a pronounced stage-cockney accent. The refrain was 'So 'ee 'umps yer, an bumps yer, an yer gits an awful 'eadache an sand gits up yer crack' and it was probably side-splittingly funny in Little Tich's day. Now it was at best a rather touching anachronism.

It was not an obvious choice for a once great classical actor stepping out from the shadows of retirement. On the other hand it had the great merit that my father knew it by heart and could recite it in his sleep. Once he had begun, I thought, it would carry him along. I was wrong.

He rose to his feet and opened his mouth. No sound came out. A waiter moved the microphone nearer to him. He peeped at his audience, his round expressive eyes in his immobile face looking shyly mischievous.

'When I was a child,' he began, his voice so choked and faint that the whole audience leaned forward to hear him, 'I used to enjoy a story about the seaside . . . like this . . .'

The pause which followed this introduction was long, and grew longer. Michael stood swaying behind his microphone, peeping mischievously about, opening and closing his lips like a goldfish. But no sound came out. The first line of his monologue remained lodged in his throat, or mangled in his memory. In that everlasting pause I too desperately searched my memory. If only I had known the first line I could have leapt to his side and jump-started him by speaking it for him. Yet I could only look on helplessly, willing him to find something – anything – to say.

Fully a minute must have passed. My father had achieved the longest unprompted 'dry' in theatrical history. Then he said, 'I think I'd better sit down, don't you?' The frailty of him, who had once been so superbly robust, and the touching dignity of his farewell moved his audience to tears. Clements, never in the least sentimental, was weeping openly. The dining-room emptied in five minutes. In what turned out to be his final public appearance he had hoped to make his audience laugh. But as things were, despite Garrick's and his own preference, he had moved them to tears.

When I think about him now, I am moved again by his dignity and his simplicity. Everything about his last years was in contradiction with his previous life. For instance, all his life he had been a notorious hypochondriac. As a child, I used to wander through his bedroom, opening drawers and cabinets stuffed with pills and potions, and complicated rubber contraptions whose purpose one could only guess as. All were related to his stomach and bowels, the workings of which he both worshipped and placated as the Philistines worshipped the god Dagon. Yet now that he was severely ill and much handicapped he never complained at all.

The reviews for his book were good. One or two were very good. But my father, who had never been indifferent to reviews as an actor, took little notice of them now. Gradually the excitement which had buoyed him up in the pre-launch period began to evaporate. Perhaps he was repeating the pattern of his life as an actor. He had always loved the preparation of a part. He once spent weeks in a cottage on the Duke of Northumberland's estate at Alnwick to learn the Northumbrian accent he wanted for Hotspur. He had enjoyed the early stage of rehearsals too. But when the first night came all enjoyment drained away and in its place came an awful ennui.

For two and a half years we had met three days a week, rain or shine, until the final chapter was written. There had been the pleasure of thinking what he would do with the next instalment of his publishers' advance, though in fact there was not so much now to spend his money on except when he went to see Alan. Then had come the thrill of seeing his autobiography in print, in page proofs, and the business of making corrections. Michael was full of arcane literary anecdotes, one of which concerned the process of correction, and was told of Oscar

Wilde. 'What did you do this morning, Oscar?' asked an admirer. 'I have fatigued myself quite dreadfully,' came the reply. 'All morning I have wrestled with a composition.' 'Yes?' said the admirer. 'What did you do?' 'I removed a comma.' That evening the same admirer met Wilde again – and again the same expression of exquisite fatigue. 'And what did you do this afternoon, Oscar?' 'I put it back.'

He had enjoyed the publicity too, especially going to New York to launch the book in America. He considered himself a citizen by adoption of New York; there, if anywhere, the spring returned to his step.

Yet even with a bunch of good reviews a writer's life must have seemed solitary and unrewarded compared with an actor's. There was scarcely any sense of an audience, and certainly not of an audience brought together by the shared experience of a play. There was little or nothing to prompt the flow of adrenalin. Without the excitement and fear which make adrenalin flow, my father grew old more quickly.

Nothing had prepared me for this swift decline. Back in Yorkshire I heard that he had been admitted to the London Hospital in Whitechapel. Professor Watkins, the neurosurgeon he had been referred to, asked him to stay in the hospital for a fortnight so that he could check Michael's medication. Sinemet is a powerful drug. Too little, and you plunge into severe depression, exhausting yourself with the trembling of your hands and legs which in the right quantity the drug controls. Too much and you hallucinate. When I came to see him he was definitely having too much. His hearing had always been acute; now it was painfully so. He heard voices whispering about him in the corridor outside his room.

'What are they saying?'

'Oh, you know, that I shouldn't have been given all this.' He gestured at the room, which was small and like most hospital rooms quite bare.

'Why not?'

'Well, you know, I shouldn't really have a room to myself.'

'Why not? You deserve it. You need it.'

'Do I? Perhaps. But we're not liked, you know. We're not popular.'

'What makes you think that?'

'That's what they're saying.' He pointed to the corridor.

I said the voices were a side effect of the Sinemet, and that whenever he heard them he should tell himself not to worry, it was only the drug talking. He brightened up at this suggestion, and promised to remember it.

I went back to Doncaster, and was relieved to be told when I next telephoned the hospital for news that he had discharged himself ahead of time. Apparently he hadn't come home either. He had hailed a cab and disappeared. Probably he's gone to find Alan, I thought. It was comforting to suppose him still independent and on the loose.

Some time later I telephoned his flat in Chelsea and spoke to Jean, who nursed him. It was the autumn of 1984. Evidently I hadn't been in touch for a while because I now learned that he had two nurses, by night as well as by day.

'I think you ought to see him,' Jean said.

It was late in the evening, almost midnight, when I arrived, but Jean was still there, which made me nervous. Michael was lying in bed with the huge tabby cat he called Dodger coiled asleep on his alarmingly distended tummy. With his eyes half closed, and with his terribly swollen tummy, he looked dreadful.

'You put the wind in my sails,' he murmured. Jean put her head around his bedroom door and beckoned me to follow her into the kitchen, where Michael's family doctor was waiting. Gently, slowly, he explained that Michael's voluntary muscles were no longer acting reliably, and this had now affected his bladder. He was being poisoned by urine retention, and unless he were taken immediately to hospital ... Here the doctor seemed to steady me before pronouncing the alternative – 'or you may feel that his disease is so far advanced that the best thing is to allow it to run its course.'

It took a moment before I realised that I was being given the power of life or death over my father. Michael must have known that this was happening, with his hyper-acute hearing and extra sensitivity. Was that why he had greeted me tonight as if I were his rescuer? I burst into tears and choked out that, no question, he must live as long as medicine and his will would keep him alive. The doctor bowed his head before my tearful tirade, reassuring me that I had made the right choice. Hours later Michael was admitted to St Bartholomew's Hospital. A catheter drained off his urine and he recovered quite quickly.

He stayed in Bart's for about a month. A special bed was provided with an electric motor which very slowly and evenly altered the plane of the mattress so that he would not suffer from bedsores. When I think of the care he received I rage against the perpetrators of 'market reforms' in the National Health Service.

After a month or so, however, the consultant specialist explained that they had done all they could for Michael. He was as well as they could make him. Now it was up to us, his children, to decide where to put him.

In January 1985 we took him to a nursing home in Denham, near the film studios where as a film star he had often worked. It was run by the Licensed Victuallers Association for the benefit of retired publicans. Peter Egan, an actor friend whose father-in-law had been nursed in a similar home, recommended it and it turned out to be an excellent choice. My father was put in a ward for four patients, opposite an old fellow called Duncan who had kept a pub in Shaftesbury Avenue and remembered my father from the wartime. Duncan was dying of emphysema, but still cheerfully smoking. He could remember Michael's war films almost word for word, and in between bouts of coughing he entertained us with scenes from *The Way to the Stars*.

Every Monday I came down from Yorkshire, and my wife Kika and I would visit him. Soon our visits developed their own pattern and ritual. My father, dressed in readiness for our arrival, would be fast asleep on his bed by the time we came. After rousing him and levering him into his wheelchair we would set off at a gallop for the bar which – this being a home for retired victuallers – was the epicentre of the nursing home. It was as well stocked as any Soho pub and just as lively, the only difference being the age of the customers and the number of wheelchairs. It would be hard to imagine a scene more English than this gathering of retired publicans drinking and smoking to their hearts' content, and my father revelled in it. It crossed my mind to wonder whether he had ever felt more at home than he seemed here, except that during lunch he would become tired and afterwards fall silent. When the time came for us to leave he would rouse himself to wave gallantly.

His birthday, on 20 March, fell on a Tuesday that year, and he was seventy-seven. I stayed in London an extra day in honour of the occasion, and would have returned to Yorkshire in the afternoon but he complained of feeling very tired and was found to have a temperature. During the afternoon his temperature rose and the nurses removed his pyjamas and all his bedclothes except a sheet. Even so he sweated and writhed in pain, so the doctor was called and said simply that they should place an electric fan next to his bed and cool him down.

Next morning, Wednesday 21 March 1985, as I entered his ward he cried out as if I'd come to torment him, and I realised he was barely conscious. He is dying, I thought. Perhaps I could still have saved him, called the doctor and insisted on antibiotics, but I just sat there talking to him, trying to comfort him with the sound of my voice.

His breathing was deep and raucous. I took out the paperback edition of his autobiography and began to read at random.

May 1940 . . . I told Rachel all about Roy and his end: always it returns to this question of a split personality, and I cannot feel it would be right – even if I had the will-power, which I have not – to cut off or starve the other side of my nature. I complained, weakly, but with some sense, that whereas people go to see plays like *Mourning Becomes Electra* and *The Family Reunion*, they nevertheless think a person morbid who feels as those characters feel and I felt last night, and have felt obscurely before, that

It is possible you are the consciousness of your unhappy family
Its bird sent flying through the purgatorial flame . . .

I turned back to the chapter about his holiday abroad in Normandy when he was sixteen. Oliver Baldwin, the Conservative Prime Minister's son, had come to stay at the same hotel, with two young men friends. Michael's passionate admiration for Oliver stands out in every paragraph. Oliver was a socialist, and fearless enough to stand for Parliament in the 1924 election in Dudley, the neighbouring constituency to his father's. After the war, when he served in the Brigade of Guards, he became actively involved in the fate of 'poor, bloody Armenia'. He had risen to the rank of lieutenant-colonel in the Armenian army and had been captured by both the Turks and the Bolsheviks, and incarcerated in six different prisons. He was writing his book *Six Prisons and Two Revolutions* when he met Michael on holiday at Veules-les-Roses.

I looked up at my father. It occurred to me that I should have tried to find Alan. Perhaps he wanted to see him.

It was too late. He took a deep painful breath, then paused, as it seemed for a long time, took one more deep breath and a sigh, and then no more.

That night we walked on Waterloo Bridge, Kika, Vanessa, Lynn, Rachel and her brother Nicholas. We were crying, laughing and joking, and there on the electronic board of the National Theatre we saw they had suspended the usual advertisements for their plays and had written 'Michael Redgrave: Actor 1908–1985'.

4

The Way In

ℜ

I was born in London on 16 July 1939, less than two months before war was declared. The house, 102 Clifton Hill, is still there, as are all the neighbouring houses in St John's Wood, undamaged by the blitz. But soon after the bombing began we moved to Bromyard, a village in Herefordshire, and when we returned to London during a lull in the bombing in 1943 it was to a flat in Putney overlooking the river, and then in 1946 to Chiswick, so I have no memories of the house where I was born, and to this day I have never seen it. Vanity perhaps prevents me – or fear of surrendering myself to nostalgia.

The photographs taken for *Picture Post* invite nostalgia: a prosperous-looking house; a chandelier, a Bechstein grand piano; 'Michael Redgrave at home'. They call him 'the film star'. It would be some years before I knew what that meant. *Picturegoer* published an annual popularity poll and his name would jostle for space above or below those of John Mills, Stewart Granger, James Mason, Michael Wilding and later Alec Guinness. But in the year I was born he was more popular than all the others. His very first film had seen to that – *The Lady Vanishes*, released in January 1939. Then came *Stolen Life*, a romance with Elizabeth Bergner. It was very popular though it has since disappeared. Bergner sweetly consented to be my godmother, and gave me a cornflower-blue leather suitcase, so soft you could caress your cheek with it, and so expensive that no one ever dreamed of using it. Next came *Climbing High* with Jessie Matthews, released in May 1939. In July, when I was born, my father was shooting *The Stars Look Down*, with Margaret Lockwood.

If there had been an equivalent of McCarthy's US Senate committee or the House Un-American Activities Committee in Britain after the war, the first thing it would have done would be to subpoena everyone connected with making *The Stars Look Down*. It makes the most persuasive case for the nationalisation of coal, all the stronger because the story is so simply and imaginatively filmed.

A coal owner has hidden the plans which show that a seam of coal is being worked dangerously close to water, with the risk that the mine will flood. The miners' leader brings them out on strike, despite the warnings of the trade-union bureaucrats who are in the pocket of the owner. The men's leader is gaoled, and they go back to work. The disaster happens. A rock fall lets tons of water into the workings, and the miners are trapped underground. The last twenty minutes show the desperate losing battle which the men above ground fight to dig their mates out.

Some fine films were made in the 1930s about the lives of working people, and one or two great films, such as *The Grapes of Wrath*. But none I think is so bold and uncompromising as *The Stars Look Down*. It does more than protest against the greed and exploitation which sent these men to their deaths. It shows that coal, the nation's wealth, which is made not by man but by nature, and yet is the foundation of all man-made wealth, must be taken out of the hands of private owners if such accidents as happen in the story are to be prevented. The central figure, played by my father, is Davy Fenwick. He starts working down the mine but gets a scholarship to university. He wants an education not so that he can lift himself above the miners but so as to argue their cause more effectively.

Michael plays him with the sort of conviction which cannot be bought or copied. You can see at once why audiences took this actor to their hearts and made him their favourite. What

he does here (as also in the 1947 film of *Fame is the Spur*)
illuminates the chief paradox of acting: simply that at its best
it ceases to be acting. I am always aware that this is Michael,
the look in his eye, the set of his shoulders and especially his
walk, which is as characteristic of him as is the walk of Henry
Fonda, the most memorable of film actors. I never cease to be
aware of him, and yet I find his personality has fused completely
with his fictional persona. He is both himself and the other of
himself. That would be difficult enough to achieve if what he
was expressing were no more than the simple decencies of the
American constitution, life, liberty and the pursuit of happiness. All of Fonda's performances constituted a set of variations
on that theme.

But Fonda was not, so far as I know, a socialist. If he had
been called before those terrible interrogators whose 'Are you
now, or have you ever been . . . ?' maimed so many lives, he
would never have needed to have taken the Fifth Amendment
unless he wanted to assert his constitutional right to silence.
My father on the other hand was a convinced and very public
socialist. He had no need to imitate Fenwick's belief that coal
must be nationalised, because it was his belief too. If a tribunal
such as HUAC had compelled him to testify 'Are you now, or
have you ever been . . . ?', the answer, in both cases, would
have been 'Yes'.

I must assert that I believe that Michael's socialist convictions
made him, at least in the specific case of *The Stars Look Down*,
all the more remarkable an actor. And I am equally certain
that that performance, and that film, helped to prepare the
climate of opinion which gave the Labour Party a landslide
victory in 1945, and enabled the government to nationalise the
mines in 1947.

I never saw *The Stars Look Down* until two years ago, when
my wife bought a video recording of the film for a birthday
present. Having my father's performance there on tape where
I could summon it late at night or at any hour I chose played
curious tricks with my recollection of him. Typically I imagine

31

him much as I suppose we all imagine our fathers, bigger, taller, stronger than myself, his cheek and chin rough to the touch, his voice deep, his smell, a mixture of tobacco and cologne, both foreign and familiar. That is to say I remember him essentially as *older*. So he appears in my dreams, though very rarely, in fact only twice since his death ten years ago.

— His beard was grizzled, no?
— It was as I have seen it in his life,
   A sable silvered.

But the man on the screen is thirty-one, not much older than my eldest son – and in his cloth cap and shirt-sleeves, his long wrists too long for his jacket, his long neck and half-awkward movements, he looks and sounds not much more than a youth. Stranger still, the young man who plays the son of the coal owner is David Markham, my wife's father; and David looks even younger. It must have been while making this film that they met for the first time, and Olive Markham knitted my mother a shawl for the baby she was carrying, me.

St Swithin's Day, 15 July, was fine that year, thus confirming the superstition that a dry summer needs a dry St Swithin, and promising the governments of Europe the early and big harvest which, according to another superstition, is the prerequisite for making war. Shooting, at Twickenham, finished early on 15 July, and my father, still in the clothes he wore as Davy Fenwick, left the studios at two o'clock. At Baker Street he stopped at a flower seller's to buy a big armful of roses, only to find he'd left his wallet in his street clothes which were still in the dressing-room at Twickenham. 'That's all right,' said the flower seller. 'Pay me tomorrow.' Thanking her profusely, and reflecting that she had probably guessed the reason for which he bought the roses, he hurried on to St John's Wood. He found my mother complaining of a chill and aching. Later that evening he read her two chapters of *Lark Rise to Candleford* and she fell asleep. But an hour later she called out that she thought she had started. The midwife came, and together

Michael and she arranged the room with oilcloth beside the bed. Then they telephoned the doctor.

All this, and much more, is noted in my father's journal. It is both flattering and fascinating to see one's birth recorded in such detail over so many pages – the more so because the book is not a diary, remorselessly jotting each day's events, but a journal, which begins in the summer of 1938 and ends with my father's release from the navy which invalided him back to civilian life early in 1942; and the entry which describes my birth and covers several pages is only the third in the book.

Flattering indeed; and yet I must also remember that my father was a disciple of Stanislavsky, whose great manual on acting, *An Actor Prepares*, enjoins his students over and again to observe life, and record their observations. I remember my father telling me that the finest acting he ever saw in the cinema was a scene in *In Which We Serve*, where Kathleen Harrison runs down a bombed-out street in London's East End laughing and screaming, 'It's a boy! She's got a boy!' As I read this account of my birth, which is utterly touching and affectionate, I see also the actor whom Stanislavsky taught to note down his feelings, simply and truthfully, so that he could, on some future occasion, as the phrase goes, 'use' them.

We decided to ring for Dr Broadbridge. He came just before 9, a charming little man in Wellington boots and tennis shirt under his mac.

I had some breakfast. Shortly after, he came down and said it was all going fine and would be over in about an hour. At first I heard nothing but feet moving about, but when I went into the hall I could hear my darling R crying with pain, not loud, high and suppressed. I wandered about, walking out into the garden, thinking the silliest thoughts, including the observation that I was watching myself, which I detested. I kept being sure it was a girl coming to forestall my disappointment. Then I heard R's voice groaning, v. low and hoarse, like an animal. Then she said, in the middle of a cry, 'I'm so sorry', which wrung my heart. The housemaid kept going up and down the stairs, as about her job. Each time I heard her coming down I thought it was the doctor or Mac [the nurse], and went into the hall, but the housemaid and I exchanged faint sad smiles. Then there was a lull, and I heard the baby crying, and thought, 'they know what it is, but I don't, I must know now, they must tell me.' And then: 'If you've been waiting as long as this you can wait a bit longer.'

There was no sound from R for some minutes and I stood in the hall. Then I heard her voice speaking, no longer in agony, and began to go upstairs. At last I couldn't wait any more, and hearing her say my name called out, 'Rachel.' Then again. Then the doctor came to the door and said I could come in: 'It's a fine boy.'

R and I hugged each other, crying with happiness and relief. And I saw him in the cot, wrapped round in a woollen sheet, wrinkled and ugly and marked with the thick paste he had been lying in. R couldn't see him from the bed and we lifted the basket down for her. Then there was some more to be done, so I went down and phoned Eric [Rachel's father], who was just going to divisions. He was wildly excited and happy. I phoned Mother, and Maud [Rachel's aunt] to tell Beatrice [Rachel's mother]. Then Robin [Rachel's younger brother]. Everyone was really excited and thrilled except Mother, and I was astonished at how calm she was, though she seemed v. pleased and there was nothing 'behind' her lack of excitement, at least nothing more than normal.

Later I saw William bathed for the first time, saw his cord tied a second time, and wrapped up in a little package on his tummy. His little tongue was bright red like a wood strawberry, and his parts seemed enormous compared to the rest of him. He weighed 8 pounds less ¼ oz.

The name William was a temporary compromise. My father wanted to call me Cornelius, but was dissuaded.

I make no other appearance in this journal until May the following year: 'Corin adorable in pram he is always cheerful.' Probably I guessed that to be anything less would risk driving him away. 'It is pleasant to watch him living a life of pure sensation: the noise of the birds, the leaves of the pear tree, the colour of the sky, the friendly loving sounds we make at him.'

He observes his children fondly but from a distance, untroubled by any particular responsibility for their nurture. He has the conventional notions of the harm which too much 'spoiling' can do, or of 'giving in' too readily to their demands or, especially harmful, paying them too much attention. Of his half-sister Peggy's son, delightfully named John Gilpin, he observes: 'very timid. Needs to be left alone more. I mean less notice taken of him.' Only once in this journal does he spend a day caring for Vanessa and me. We are at our cousin Lucy's in Herefordshire. Our nurse has the day off, and Rachel has been summoned at short notice to London for a film test at Ealing Studios. Michael's description of that day is full of the gentle, unmalicious self-mockery which as an actor he was master of.

> Corin won't eat much breakfast. He likes everything to be in order and can't make out why I'm there . . . Vanessa keeps saying she is getting a cold like Corin. I say 'rubbish'. She also insists that she has something in her toe. I also say 'rubbish' to this. But after the fourth time I say 'all right then, take your shoe and sock off and see what it is.' It is a large thorn.

What with the war, his service in the navy, and after the navy his work, mostly in London, in theatre and films, I have very few memories of my father at this early stage of my childhood. Circumstances conspired to repeat in my childhood his own experiences of his father, or rather his lack of them. Roy had deserted Michael's mother when he was two and a half years old. To be strictly accurate, Roy didn't actually desert her. Daisy gave up the unequal struggle of pursuing him across Australia, all too often arriving at the hotel after he had just left and then being unable to leave herself until she had paid his bill as well as her own.

Roy, whom my father never knew, had a larger influence over his son's life than any father who deserted his child at such a tender age could reasonably expect. He became the pattern of what not to do; he who at all costs must never be copied, even unconsciously. 'Once,' his mother wrote to him, 'when you were quite small, you pointed your middle finger at me just like him and I almost screamed.'

To have one parent who deserts his offspring is unfortunate. To have another, as Lady Bracknell might have said, is . . . but no. His mother didn't desert Michael. She did the next worst thing, which was to desert her own father, and, suffering the full torment of guilt thereafter, she made sure that all that guilt, her own and Roy's, be weighed, measured and loaded on to my father's slender upright frame. If he, thereafter, should from time to time stumble under so much weight, who could blame him? And is it really a question of blame at all?

The story of Daisy's desertion of her father is so extraordinary that no Edwardian melodrama, not even the melodramas which Roy himself wrote in profusion, piled high with coincidence, and always with fat parts for himself, could do justice to it. She had left home, in Portsmouth, aged fifteen, to try her luck in London as an actress. She took herself to the offices in Maiden Lane of one St John Denton, a successful theatrical agent – so successful, in fact, that the stairs to his first-floor office were lined with actors hoping to audition for him, and she had to trick her way past the queue by pretending she had a message for him. Daisy found herself in the great man's presence and sang him two songs, Blake's 'Jerusalem' and 'Merry Goes the Heart'. He sat po-faced through the first, but laughed and clapped at the second, and asked her name. She said her name was Daisy Scudamore, whereat he laughed some more and said, 'You must be little Scudie's daughter.' She wasn't, of course. She was the daughter of William Scudamore, wainwright, of 8 Victory Villas, Portsmouth; or so she thought. But 'Scudie' sounded like someone who might help her, so she asked his address and went to call on him in Castlenau, Barnes.

Fortunatus Augustus Scudamore, commonly shortened to 'F.A.', opened the front door to her. He was quite successful, as his substantial house in this suburb indicated, as a character actor, and more so as the actor-manager and author of popular

dramas like *Betrayed!* Before she had said a word of explanation he had flung his arms around her, exclaiming, 'If you
are not my daughter, I don't know whose daughter you may
be.' (I have copied the line word for word from my grandmother's notebook, the same in which she wrote her warning
to Michael.)

Daisy was welcomed into the house, as F.A.'s daughter, by
his understanding wife and his son Lionel, also an actor, of
whom Daisy grew very fond. Together they acted all round
London, but chiefly at Mile End, in F.A.'s plays. He doted on
her, and wrote all his *ingénue* roles for her.

One afternoon, however, there was a family argument, with
F.A. scolding Lionel for something or other. Daisy took her
brother's side and at the climax of the argument stormed out
of the house, threatening that she would not perform in his
play that night.

She did, of course. But to underline her side of the argument
she stayed away from home after the performance, and the
next night, so that almost forty-eight hours had passed before
she turned her key in the lock of the front door at Castlenau.
The door wouldn't open. Nor would the back door, the trades-
men's door, nor any of the windows, most of which were
curtained. When the police opened up, they found no signs of
disturbance, until they came to F.A.'s study. The walls were
covered with drawings, photographs and theatre posters. F.A.
lay dead at the foot of a stepladder. He had turned all the
photographs of Daisy, and any poster on which her name
appeared, to the wall – all but one, which was so high he must
have needed to stand on tiptoe to reach it. Perhaps it was the
act of reaching up to this last photograph which had precipi-
tated his heart attack. Or perhaps he just lost his balance and
fell from the stepladder.

His mother's warnings to Michael that he should on no
account take after his father were on the face of it successful.
Michael never deserted us. Although from time to time, and
only when the going got very rough, my mother suggested a

separation, she never persisted because the mere mention of it brought such a storm of grief that she had to spend the rest of the week comforting him. On the other hand I have no doubt that a good deal of the wanderer in Roy rubbed off on his son.

I have only two memories of my father from this time of early childhood, both of which tell me that he might have been a marvellous parent if only he had known how. In the first memory he has come to stay with us on one of his flying visits to Herefordshire. He is carrying me across a stream, like St Christopher. To cross it we must walk along a narrow plank. He crosses it and beckons me from the other side. I set one foot on it, but dare not go further, so he comes back and hoists me on his shoulders. The second is of a night not long before the end of the war – or perhaps from that period of respite in the bombing of London, after the mass raids and before the V1 rockets. It is no more than a snapshot. My father is sitting on the edge of my bed. I have woken with a cough and he has brought me a mug of blackcurrant cordial.

I envied my sister terribly at this time. He called her 'Van', and they used to paint together, and she was allowed to see his plays, whereas I was too young. She told me about his acting, but I had no idea what she meant, nor of what he actually did for a living. When I was almost six I was taken to the Piccadilly Theatre to see him in a play called *Jacobowsky and the Colonel* by Franz Werfel. I remember nothing except a pistol shot which frightened the life out of me, and a dull dissatisfaction that during the entire afternoon I failed to recognise my father.

My first visit to the cinema was equally disappointing. In 1946 we were taken to *The Captive Heart*. I felt sure this would go better because everyone was talking about it. Mr Owen the gardener had seen it. Ron the greengrocer who drove an electric van piled high with Brussels sprouts had seen it. Mrs Graham who had the sweetshop and post office on the corner had seen it. My teacher at my new primary school in Sutton Court Road in Chiswick had seen it, and all the parents of all the boys in my class, who thought I was such an oddity that they stuck pencils in my cheeks to see if I was real. But as far as I was concerned it was nearly as complete a failure as *Jacobowsky and the Colonel*. Halfway through the film I noticed my father, in an enormous close-up. He was kneeling on the ground holding a wooden stake which another man was hammering into the earth. My father rested his hand on top of the stake, down came the hammer – and I let out a loud wail. After that one, agonising moment, I never spotted him again, and only much later did I find out that my mother had an important part in the film as his penfriend and sweetheart.

Next I was taken to see *Macbeth*. I was eight years old, and I sat with Edith Hargraves, my father's secretary, in the front row of the dress circle of the Aldwych Theatre. In case yet another afternoon should pass without my spotting him I begged her to nudge me every time he appeared. After a few scenes I was black and blue with her nudges. She was a dear, boisterous woman. The trouble was, there were a great many people on the stage and all of them speaking at once. After a while, however, I noticed that one of them was taller than all the rest, and also spoke a great deal more, and, since I knew my father always played the main part and was by far the tallest man I had ever seen, I figured this must be he. I knew he would ask me what I thought of his performance, so I tried hard to pay attention.

The man in question had very long hair, like a hermit, and piercing eyes. He certainly spoke a great deal. Sometimes all the other actors would walk off the stage, leaving him alone, and still he carried on talking, just talking to himself. Now and again he seemed to have difficulty pronouncing the words, which was not surprising because a great deal of what he had to say was in a foreign language. Once he made a mistake and said the same word twice.

I was taken round to his dressing-room in the interval.

'What did you think?'

'Very good. You only made one mistake.'

'What was that?'

'You said the same word twice.'

'Which word?'

'Success. You said, "Success, success".'

'No. I said, ". . . and catch with his surcease, success".'

Then it was time to go back. The second half was a great deal more exciting. A green man suddenly appeared from nowhere and sat in a chair next to my father, who roared at him. Edith explained in a whisper that the green man was a ghost. And then came the most thrilling part by far. My father drew his sword. I had been waiting for this for a long time, knowing there was to be a fight. His opponent was almost as tall as himself, but I was in no doubt who would win. And then calamity. My father had to walk backwards up a staircase, fighting all the while, and suddenly he tripped, and before he could get up it was all over. The other man had won.

'Bad luck,' I said. I felt awful about that and wanted to go home.

'I tripped on purpose,' said my father. 'I did it specially for you. I thought it would make it more exciting.'

I begged to see *Macbeth* again and again, and for a long time all my ideas of acting and the theatre were shaped by this play, whole chunks of which I came to know by heart. I particularly liked the weird sisters, who were also easier to understand than the others. But I managed to enjoy even what I could not understand, and took to chanting some of the most incomprehensible phrases, like mantras: 'Blood-boltered Banquo', 'shard-born beetle', 'the multitudinous seas incarnadine, making the green one red'.

Soon afterwards I was sent to boarding-school, and in the depth of night, in the winter term, when I heard the train down in the valley going from Malvern to Worcester, and hoped to be on that train, I comforted myself with whispered phrases from *Macbeth*. 'All hail, Macbeth! Hail to thee, Thane of Glamis!' and then, darkly, 'All hail, Macbeth! Hail to thee, Thane of Cawdor!' And finally, mysterioso, 'All hail, Macbeth, that shalt be king hereafter.' To repeat so much by heart made me feel both clever and important, possessing a knowledge none other of the sleeping bodies in my dormitory had at their command.

It was 10 May 1949. I should have been away at prep school, at Wells House. The summer term had begun more than a week before; yet with the start of each new term I was finding it harder to control my tears. This was to be my fourth term at Wells House, but two nights before I was due to return, sitting in the drawing-room with my mother and realising that I would not see her again for three months, I began to say, 'Tomorrow is the last day of the holidays', and found I couldn't complete the sentence.

For a week or so I remained at home on the pretext of being in quarantine for chicken-pox. My father took me to see an old friend, an émigrée Viennese psychiatrist called Charlotte Wolff. She was the author of a pioneering study, *The Psychology of Gesture*, and I remember that she took prints of my hands. I wasn't told why, nor why for that matter I was being taken to consult this dear, serious little woman, who gave me weak tea and chocolate biscuits and said, now and then, with a strong Viennese accent, '*Ach*! So-o interesting!', in a way which flattered me greatly though I couldn't say why.

It is quite terrifying to me now, as a father, to review this period of my life, which I know, because I can still remember its emotions so vividly, to have been among the most turbulent of my childhood. Terrifying, but salutary, because as I read my father's diary I see how little my grief seems to have impinged upon him. And I cannot help accusing myself of the countless times I must myself have been ignorant of my children's grief.

'Corin said to be in tears in evening at thought of going back,' says his diary on 12 May. 'Said to be'? And the next day: 'Corin very upset. Talk to him firmly. Nearly miss train and forget to give him his ticket.'

Yes, but I remember that train ride, the most miserable of my life. Sweets were, for a brief while, no longer rationed, and I had a bar of Cadbury's Caramello in my pocket. Yet I was so sick with nerves at the thought of returning to school, and with the added problem of having no ticket, that I couldn't eat it. As I think about that terrible day now it seems to me that it should have burned a hole in the universal calendar, let alone my own father's diary. But no – his day continued normally, even cheerfully:

> Nearly miss train and forget to give him his ticket. He forgets (?) his cello. Nanny rings school as I leave for fittings. Hear from Cecil [his agent] that Rank Group agrees. Wire Hugh Hunt [director of the Old Vic]. A good performance. Home to supper. Tired. Plant lavender in the front, also tomatoes.

I had looked forward to boarding-school, and somehow it had never occurred to me that I might feel lonely or homesick. When I first arrived I achieved an instant popularity, on the strength of expectations – did I know Jane Russell? could I get Stewart Granger's autograph? – which were soon disappointed. Even though I could never recapture the buzz of excitement which greeted my arrival as the son of a famous film star, there was some comfort in finding, after that first wave of factitious popularity had subsided, that I could still make friends and get along.

Yet as winter term succeeded summer, and spring winter, I found the end of each holiday more unbearably poignant, and the beginning of each term more leadenly dispiriting than the last, and it dawned upon me that boarding-school was not the paradise for boys which my imagination had painted in advance but a hellish, cruel trap, a sort of labour camp, or worse, with remissions, which were the cruellest thing of all, because they gave you a taste of home and its comforts only to tear you away.

'Talk to him firmly' is a chilling phrase in my father's diary, but it meant, so far as I can recall, that I was given a promise that if I still didn't like my school by half-term I should not have to go back the following term. My father explained – and this I can remember clearly because even then I was aware of his financial worries – that it would be extremely expensive to him if I were to leave school then and there, without a term's notice.

He was as good as his word. He appeared in June, at half-term, the first and last time he ever visited the school.

'That's a very nice suit,' I told him.

He said it was for a film, *The Astonished Heart*, which he had decided not to do. He had given up his part to Noël Coward, who had written the screenplay, an adaptation of one of his short stage plays.

We watched a cricket match in which the school's First XI played the staff. Then my father left me and strode round the cricket pitch with the headmaster. He looked angry and strained when he returned.

'Do you still want to leave at the end of this term?' he asked me.

'I'm afraid I do,' I said.

'Good. All right, then.'

My father seemed almost pleased, and much later I found out that he was very relieved. The headmaster, as all of us boys knew, was a crank and a sadist, though he had obviously convinced a few generations of parents, including my mother, that his methods were sound and wholesome. When my father informed him that I was not happy he was furious, and said it was the first time he had ever been told such a thing – though it didn't surprise him in my case because I was clearly neurasthenic and educationally subnormal, as would be seen in my score in the IQ test. Intelligence testing was still more or less in its infancy but Mr Darvall was proud to pioneer it at Wells House.

I was always grateful to my father for taking me away, and still am. Yet it seemed to me I had failed. The whole experience of school thereafter remained frightening. But what was there that I could complain of? I had made my protest and got my way, and, if now I found that even day-school – although certainly preferable to boarding-school – was still a sombre and distressing place, to whom should I complain?

5

No Life for a Man

✪

'Acting', my grandmother used to say, was 'no life for a man'. What she meant, I think, was that an actor could not be relied upon to earn enough to support a wife. And even if he did he was likely to be unfaithful to her. To be manly, in her view, was to be honest, loyal, industrious and truthful – all virtues which my grandfather Roy conspicuously lacked.

It is hard to imagine the extent to which her view of life, combining truths and truisms which had been sanctified in the reign of Dr Arnold and institutionalised by Baden-Powell, existed as a broad consensus throughout the late Victorian, Edwardian and Georgian eras. Yet I find it almost impossible to understand my grandparents without submitting a little to its influence. It is the moral template for almost all Wilde's satire, exploiting the contradiction between the fascination of what we fear is evil and the boredom of what we believe is good. Wilde would have found some irony in my grandmother's plight. Though she broke with Roy after two years of marriage she was miserable to learn that he had 'taken up with another', and never ceased to pine for him.

Roy Redgrave is to my mind the most beguiling character in this whole company. I once made an attempt to write a film script about him to be called 'Roy and Daisy', and there are plenty of good acting parts in it, all of which I fear I might be too old to play by the time my film is made. Daisy was born around 1880 and when she met Roy in 1907 he was thirty-five. But I shall return to Roy later.

'Flotsam and jetsam' my grandmother called him, but added that 'everyone was mad about Roy – men loved him and women adored him.' She even pursued him beyond the grave (he died in poverty aged fifty in Sydney in 1922) with the aid of a spiritualist medium. Andy, on the other hand, whom she wooed and won to gain a home for herself and a father for her children, bored her to tears. And Andy was stuffed with manly virtues.

Daisy changed her name to Margaret after she married Andy. I am not sure when the change occurred. Perhaps it was when she played Lady Bracknell in a modern-dress revival of *The Importance of Being Earnest*. It was one of the many changes, large and small, which accompanied the move to Chapel Street, Belgravia.

Marriage to Andy meant that Michael could be given an expensive education. Despite her socialism, which was more Fabian than egalitarian, this was her dearest wish, as it was for generations of actors whose social status, notoriously, was no higher than that of 'rogues and vagabonds'. So Michael went to preparatory school in London, public school at Clifton, half a year at Heidelberg, half a year on the Loire near Tours, and four years, including a postgraduate year, at Magdalene College, Cambridge. All of this was on the unspoken understanding that he was not intended to follow in the footsteps of his father Roy. Nothing was said or written to prevent his becoming an actor. Yet the moral force of his parents' prejudices acted on him like a charm. Witness his diary entry, on the last day of his last term at Clifton, in the summer of 1926:

I saw the Headmaster on Friday morning. He was very nice and I quite liked him for once.

'You're going in for publishing, aren't you?'

I said I hoped so.

'No inclinations to go on the stage?'

None whatever.

Still he shouldn't be surprised to see me there soon. Oh! Yes! he knew I probably disliked the idea now but ... well ... we should see. He had been to school with Nicholas Hannen. Had acted together. Hannen used to repudiate the idea of the stage ... However, best of luck!

There would be nothing remarkable about this if Michael had had for any reason an aversion to acting. But he clearly adored it, though there were many other interests, especially music and singing. In this, the diary of his last term, he lists all the parts he has played at Clifton: beginning with the second niece in Sheridan's *The Critic*, graduating to the leading women's parts, Lady Mary in Barrie's *The Admirable Crichton*, Mrs Hardcastle in Goldsmith's *She Stoops to Conquer*, Lady Macbeth, and finally to Captain Absolute in Sheridan's *The Rivals*, 'which I decided to take, as Bob Acres, though a better part, is horribly short'.

Nothing was done to discourage him from acting, at either school or university. His mother, though never his stepfather, went to Bristol for three of his performances. Of his Lady Macbeth she wrote, about the sleepwalking scene, 'You not only really seemed to be asleep, you bowed your head at the end of the scene and your head seemed to drop as if you were tired to death. It was a lovely bit of business.' This was written years later in one of her notebooks, school exercise books which Michael had sent her, suggesting that since she remembered so much about the theatre of her days it should be recorded. 'Don't write what you thought of this or that actor or actress,' he advised, 'so much as what you were paid, working conditions, landladies, Sunday "train calls" and the rest of it.'

She filled five of his exercise books and these – together with every letter she ever received from Roy, bound up in two hatboxes marked 'Woollands, Knightsbridge', where in palmier days she used to buy her clothes – were duly sent to my father after her death in 1958 in the nursing home in Stanmore where she ended her days.

They are a strange curiosity shop of memories and reflections. And if at first one is assaulted by the strong smell of camphor, which they, like most theatrical memoirs, seem to exhale, they soon begin to exert an ambiguous, disturbing charm, as do vintage collections of dolls and dolls' houses, puppets and, in my experience, theatre museums. Here is the young girl defying her working-class parents in Portsmouth and running away to seek her fortune on the stage. Here is that young girl, three years later, surviving on £1 a week, walking on as a lady's maid to Queen Gertrude in *Hamlet*, and as a guest at the ball in *La Dame aux Camélias*, when the great Sarah Bernhardt came to London. Her description of Bernhardt dying as Hamlet, and crawling over to Gertrude to cradle her head in his/her lap, half singing a lullaby and stroking her waist-length golden hair, is beautiful.

All these diaries and letters are now in my possession and I have read them more times than I can count. Despite my father's advice, she doesn't, of course, refrain from passing judgement on those she saw and worked with, and thankfully so, because her comments, like her descriptions of Michael's sleepwalking scene, are always keenly observed.

As for her acting I have no record, unless one counts the reviews which she pasted in exercise books, and a few scattered remarks by her contemporaries. She was a leading actress in the provinces when she met Roy, though like him she never managed to appear in leading roles in the West End. (Roy billed himself as 'the dramatic cock o' the north', which meant North-East London, at the Britannia, Hoxton.) Like Roy she would complain that a charmed circle surrounded the West End and the theatres of the Trees and the Alexanders, and that a kind of freemasonry kept out actresses like herself. Later on this freemasonry, if it existed, seemed to accept her, though not in leading roles. She was a good friend of Lilian Baylis, who famously managed the Old Vic Theatre from 1914 to

1937, and she had something of her friend's great zeal for well-made popular Shakespearian and Elizabethan theatre. She started a society called the 'Fellowship of Players', which produced, incredibly, all the plays of Beaumont and Fletcher, anonymous Elizabethan plays, and texts like *Fratricide Punished*, a pirated version of *Hamlet* which was said to have been played on the Continent in Shakespeare's time. But when I saw her for the first and last time, as the Nurse in *The Young Elizabeth*, the disappointment and frustrations of her mature years had settled into something which even then was disparagingly known as 'the grand manner'.

Daisy was large and loud and wore a dead fox slung across her shoulders. She called our nanny 'Nurse', which irritated me because it sounded so pretentious, and Vanessa 'Van', which infuriated me. She had a gruff, gravelly voice which she blamed on all the Grand Guignol melodramas she had been forced to scream in as an *ingénue*, but which in fact had far more to do with whisky.

She had begun drinking heavily soon after setting up house with Andy in Chapel Street, Belgravia. Drink destroyed her personality and character, but it seems to have pickled and even preserved her body far longer than anyone who so abused herself had a right to expect. When we were growing up, her arrivals at our house in Chiswick were either ducal, heralded by days of anxious arrangements, or nightmarish. In the latter case there would be a loud imperious rapping on the door at two-thirty in the morning followed by muffled expletives which we strained to hear from our bedrooms at the top of the house, followed by an ambulance, which drove her back to Stanmore.

As a child and a young man Michael adored her. His letters to her are extravagant in their affection, as to a lover – 'My own . . .', 'My sweetheart . . .' At sixteen on holiday in France he wrote in his diary: 'Poor mother, how thankful she must have been not to have to come away with us. But how I missed her! How I missed her warm soft breast, athrob with sympathy, on which to lean my head and take comfort after a bitter

49

conflict with one of father's idiosyncrasies.' From the time of his marriage in 1935, however, her drinking became more uncontrollable. Several cures were attempted, with which she would always co-operate, or so it seemed, only to subvert them just when they seemed to promise success. Eventually my father had to commit her to a nursing home, where a strict, cruel regime of temperance was forced upon her. But even there he found her hiding half-bottles of brandy beneath the mattress. A horrible undignified struggle would ensue. She would pursue him down the corridor, evading her nurses and captors, standing on the front steps as he drove away, screaming at him, naked.

He never breathed a word in criticism of her until long after her death. On the night before her memorial service, at the actors' church in St Paul's, Covent Garden, he sat down at the piano and began to play a setting of a poem by Walter de la Mare, I think by E. J. Moeran. His eyes poured with tears in a long continuous stream, but he continued playing.

I attended my grandmother's memorial service but remember very little except that the lesson was read by Robert Atkins, a much-loved figure in his day. He was the actor-director of the Regent's Park Open Air Theatre. He had a very plummy voice, much imitated in a profession that loves eccentric voices, and towards the end of his life, which he was near by the time my grandmother died, his voice had become almost completely incomprehensible – and this made us love him all the more.

By degrees, the realisation dawned upon Andy that his attempts to provide a respectable career for his stepson were costing him in hard cash far more than the worst excesses which acting could ever indulge. While at Cambridge my father founded and edited a literary magazine called *The Venture*. It published new writing by authors who were, or would become, very distinguished: notably by Anthony Blunt, whose essays 'Self-

ABOVE LEFT MR's father, Roy Redgrave, in a costume drama

ABOVE MR's mother, Daisy Scudamore

BELOW LEFT MR in his sailor hat, in 1911

BELOW Andy (second from left) in family group

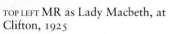

TOP LEFT MR as Lady Macbeth, at Clifton, 1925

ABOVE RIGHT MR with his stepfather, Andy

RIGHT Oliver Baldwin, in 1923

TOP LEFT With Arthur Marshall as the female lead in *Captain Brassbound's Conversion*, at the Amateur Dramatic Club in Cambridge

TOP RIGHT Anthony Blunt dressed as a woman, Cambridge, 1931

ABOVE Degree Day at Cambridge, 1931, MR, MR's mother, Andy and Viscount Falkland

LEFT MR at the piano, 1920s

RIGHT MR and Rachel
Kempson in *Flowers of
the Forest*, Liverpool
Playhouse, 1935

LEFT Rachel Kempson as
Ariel in *The Tempest*,
1934

TOP LEFT Portrait of Rachel Kempson by Cecil Beaton

TOP RIGHT MR with Rachel Kempson at Liverpool, 1935, an engagement photograph

ABOVE MR and Rachel Kempson's wedding day, Royal Naval College, Dartmouth, 18 July 1935

MR as Orlando and Edith Evans as Rosalind in *As You Like It*, the Old Vic, 1936

ABOVE RIGHT MR with Peggy Ashcroft in *The Three Sisters*, 1938

RIGHT MR as Laertes and Laurence Olivier as Hamlet in *Hamlet*, the Old Vic, 1937

OPPOSITE ABOVE MR with Margaret Lockwood, Dame May Whitty and Basil Radford in *The Lady Vanishes*, 1938

OPPOSITE BELOW MR and Diana Wynward in *Kipps*, 1941

TOP LEFT MR and Bob Michell in Hollywood, 1947

TOP RIGHT Bob Michell

RIGHT MR in bathing suit, 1930s

consciousness in Modern Art' and 'John Michael Fischer and the Bavarian Rococo' are beautifully written and highly original. But it ended after two years and six editions, leaving a large bill unpaid to its printers, R. I. Severs.

So when in 1934, after four years at Cambridge, and three as a schoolmaster teaching modern languages at Cranleigh, Michael handed in his notice and went for an audition at the Old Vic, Andy seemed not at all put out, even rather relieved. 'He had been salmon fishing all that month in Scotland and had had much luck, and due to that he did not seem to mind very much' was his mother's explanation. It would be convenient if I could leave him there, J. P. Anderson, fly-fishing in Scotland. But in fact he plays a more important part in shaping my father's destiny, and mine, than would at first appear.

Once Michael had begun his professional career upon the stage, at Liverpool Playhouse in 1934, the immediate source of friction between himself and his stepfather disappeared. He became financially independent. Even as a schoolmaster at Cranleigh he had relied upon Andy to pay his debts; but in Liverpool, with a salary of £4 a week, he managed to live on his own resources.

It almost didn't happen like that. The audition at the Old Vic had not gone particularly well, or so it seemed. He had been asked to present himself at 10.40 in the morning; they were hoping to audition six actors an hour, and he would be one of a crowd. He had chosen the prologue from *Henry IV, Part 2*, spoken by Rumour:

> Open your ears; for which of you will stop
> The vent of hearing when loud Rumour speaks?

Not a bad beginning if your audience of three is slumped in dyspeptic stupor, buried in the darkness of the stalls – as well they might be if they were auditioning twenty-four actors in a morning. Having made them sit up, though, the next thing was to keep them upright. For this Michael decided to use his height, which his mother had always insisted was a handicap. The next four lines were not only spoken fortissimo but energetically danced, with sudden lunges and soaring, sweeping movements of the hands.

> I, from the orient to the drooping west,
> (Making the wind my post-horse) still unfold
> The acts commenced on this ball of earth;
> Upon my tongue continual slanders ride,
> The which in every language I pronounce,
> Stuffing the ears of men with false reports.

At this moment a virtuoso mime was planned, in which Michael darted about the stage, whispering in a dozen different languages into the ears of an imaginary multitude, when –

'Can't you do anything else?'

Lilian Baylis herself came waddling down the aisle of the stalls.

'It's very nice, dear. But you're all hands. I can't see anything but hands.'

He launched into the opening lines of Milton's *Samson Agonistes*, which he had directed at school the previous year, taking the part of Samson himself: 'A little onward lead thy guiding hand . . .'

Too late he realised that this also, with Samson eyeless in Gaza, shuffling forward with arms outstretched, involved quite a busy use of his hands.

'You'll have to learn to use your hands, you know,' she said, adding, 'and I couldn't pay you anything. I have to pay the actors who carry the show.'

Lilian Baylis was well known for trying to get her actors for nothing, or next to nothing. But that was no great discouragement. My father would have been happy to come to the Old Vic for three shillings a week, or three pence, if it meant he would be there as a professional actor.

'I'll come,' he said bravely, 'provided you can give me something to do. I'm too old to carry spears.'

Yet nothing more was said; and for a fortnight nothing was

heard. He went to stay with a friend, and on the last day of his holiday, on his way to Cranleigh to serve out his notice in the summer term, he called at his parents' house in Chapel Street and found a letter from the Old Vic, promising him a contract for £3 a week. With this in his pocket, he caught a train at midday to Liverpool, and went for an interview with William Armstrong, the director of the Liverpool Playhouse (the former Liverpool Repertory Theatre).

Armstrong was polite but not hopeful. His autumn season was chosen, and his company was almost complete. But of course, he said, 'I'll let you know.'

'Could you let me know soon? You see, I have a contract with the Old Vic,' Michael said, reaching for the envelope in his inside pocket. That did the trick.

'How much are they paying you?'

'Three pounds a week.'

'I'll give you four pounds.'

My father knew he would play better and more varied parts in Liverpool, which was then the best repertory in the country. But it was that £4 which decided it. He rented rooms in Falkner Street and hired a piano. And at the end of his first season at Liverpool he married my mother, Rachel Kempson, who had come to the Playhouse halfway through the year on a salary of £6 a week. (She had had two years' professional experience, which included playing Juliet at Stratford-upon-Avon.) Then he was promoted, for the second season, to a salary of £8 a week. It was not a huge amount to be married with, certainly not to start a family, but it was independence, and he managed to live without serious debt.

After two years at Liverpool Playhouse they went to London, to the Old Vic, and in the autumn of 1936 they played Ferdinand and the Princess of France in *Love's Labour's Lost*. Michael was given leading parts all through the 1936–7 season, and his salary of £20 a week was the same as they paid to the season's stars, Laurence Olivier and Edith Evans. The roles he played were Orlando in *As You Like It*, Mr Horner in *The*

Country Wife and Laertes in *Hamlet*. In January 1937 Vanessa was born.

During the following season he played at the Queen's Theatre, in John Gielgud's company, with Peggy Ashcroft and Alec Guinness. He was paid £30 a week, and they moved to a flat in Moscow Road. Then, while he was playing in Chekhov's *Three Sisters* at the Queen's, he did a film test at the old Islington Studios, and was offered a contract with Gainsborough Pictures, starting with *The Lady Vanishes*, at what must then have been an enormous salary of £150 a week.

From now on Andy almost disappears from the picture in so far as his appearances in my father's diaries and letters are rare and brief. He had occupied paragraph after paragraph in the first diaries, those written at Clifton. He was the rock against which my father, in a fury, continually hurled his lance.

Andy liked to be referred to as 'The Captain' or 'Captain Anderson', though his wartime captaincy in the army was not especially noteworthy. He was very wealthy, and enjoyed using his money to make a splash and entertain. A thoroughly conventional man, Andy prided himself that he lived his life according to what were then, in the circles he moved in, the accepted standards and conventions. Once, at Chapel Street, he met my father coming out of the lavatory with a copy of *The Times*, *his* copy, which he had been vainly searching for during the last five minutes.

'A man would be thrown out of my club for doing that,' he said, snatching his paper from Michael.

He and Michael were scarcely on speaking terms, and when they did occasionally converse it was a dialogue of mutual incomprehension. 'You know, Michael,' he said one day, shaking his head sadly, 'you and I just don't talk the same language.'

Yet my mother remembers him as 'rather sweet', whereas her mother-in-law seemed a drunken bore, interminably lecturing the company on the great performers of the past, and letting it be seen all too clearly that no actress wife of Michael's could expect anything but to be eclipsed by the blazing talent of the Scudamores.

Andy's last appearance in my father's diaries, during the early part of the war, is in this altogether gentler light.

> I sit on the lawn behind the house writing this, and the shadow of the yew hedge round the rose garden has rolled itself like a dark carpet all across the lawn. I don't dare face the wireless news (6 p.m.). The others have been listening to it, and now Andy, with hat and stick, sits far away at the other end of the lawn. An impressive character.

That also is how I remember him, on the only two occasions I remember meeting him. The first was a few days after we had moved to Bedford House, a large eighteenth-century building in Chiswick Mall, in the summer of 1946. Andy and Margaret came to see the house – or rather Margaret did, because Andy by now was almost blind, although I did not understand this at the time. I remember my father calling him 'Daddy' and thinking that that was strange, because he wasn't. My father spoke to him very gently and respectfully, placing a rug over his legs when he sat on the lawn, and making sure he was not in direct sunlight.

The second occasion followed soon after, at his house in Draycott Place, Kensington. Vanessa and I were invited. My memory of this event is almost unnaturally clear. Vanessa was upstairs, talking to Margaret. I was shown down to a sitting-room in the basement of the house, where Andy sat in a high-backed leather armchair. The curtains were drawn, though it was daytime, and the only source of light was a standard lamp by Andy's head. It was only then that I fully realised that he was blind, because I kept trying to show him something – what? – and he kept repeating, 'I can't see it.' Even then it was a moment or two before I comprehended, with a shock and terrible embarrassment, that he really couldn't see what I was holding in front of his face.

This scene has now acquired for me strong overtones of

another, earlier scene, in which my father was bidden to go downstairs, sit on Uncle Andy's knee, 'and call him Daddy'. Except, of course, Andy is now blind; and except also for the further detail which softens this last memory. I was waiting for my grandmother to come and terminate this interview, and like Andy I had run out of things to say. Suddenly Andy said, 'I'll show you how I wiggle my ears.' I looked closely at his very large mottled ears, but for the life of me I could not see even a twitch.

'There!' said Andy. 'Did you see?'

'Yes,' I said, dutifully, 'I think so.'

Much later when I read Carson McCullers's *The Ballad of the Sad Café*, in which the dwarf Cousin Lymon can wiggle his ears, I thought of Andy.

Andy died on 18 March 1947, while my father was in Hollywood filming a thriller, *The Secret Beyond the Door*, directed by his friend Fritz Lang. The script was poor, and would have benefited, if anything could have helped it, from that fast, blunt style of shooting, without frills, which we associate with 'B-movies' from Monogram. It certainly wasn't helped by Lang's obsessive, meticulous attention to detail.

After Andy's death my grandmother recalled their first night out together. Leaving Michael in the care of the housekeeper at their digs in Faunce Street, Kennington, she put on her best dress and took a taxi to the Trocadero in Piccadilly. She was late, of course, and in a hurry. As the taxi pulled up outside the restaurant she realised that she didn't have anything near enough money to pay the fare. 'I imagined having to pawn something, and how difficult that would be. But Andy, good man, paid it for me.'

That understated parenthesis, 'good man', stayed with my father for the rest of his life. He used to repeat it to himself if ever – which was rare, it's true – the subject of Andy arose, as if that little phrase helped him finally to exorcise all the ungrateful thoughts he had had as a boy.

We all found reason to be grateful to him. Quite often he

rescued us when the going was rough. It was exceptionally rough for my father in the early 1950s. He had played two seasons at Stratford in 1951 and 1953 on what was even then a low salary. He was also extravagant and generous and highly imprudent in everything to do with his finances. His notions of economy were bizarre, like raging about the house switching off lights, and were often followed by a fit of wild extravagance. By 1954 he was insolvent, and only saved from actual bankruptcy by his agent, who now took over the management of his career and dictated a stream of film parts, some good, some very mediocre.

My father was pacing up and down the lawn. He had come home early that day from the studios where he was filming *The Dam Busters*. He had dyed his hair white for the part of the scientist who invented the bouncing bomb, Barnes Wallis. I knew he was worried about money, though I couldn't understand why, because he was making one film after another. I used to lie awake at night dreaming up schemes to rescue him from his financial difficulties though I couldn't understand what they were, nor why they made my father walk with his shoulders hunched forward as now.

'Are you all right?' I asked.

My father said he was very relieved. He told me that he had just found out that Andy, before his death, had set up a trust which could be used, among other possibilities, for his grandchildren's education.

'Oh, that's good,' I said.

I had had no idea that my education had been at risk. I was at Westminster School, and not greatly enjoying it that year, and felt that I would not at all have minded if I had been taken away.

It wasn't only my father and our education that Andy rescued. He even rescued me. It was the early 1980s, and I had become a full-time political organiser for the Workers' Revolutionary Party, which meant that I had been doing no professional acting for some time. Yet I had an overdraft of £5,000 and the bank manager had had enough of my excuses and promises as to when it would be paid off. I was on the point of surrendering, when a letter arrived from Grindlays Bank in St James's Square informing me that the late (by now very late) J. P. Anderson had left a sum of money, by now almost £10,000. For some reason, which embarrassed everyone at Grindlays, this had been overlooked, the letter told me, but it was clearly intended for me.

Even now it sometimes occurs to me to hope or wonder whether the long arm of Captain Anderson may not reach me in distress and pull me to the shore.

6

Are You Now or Have You Ever Been?

☙

At some time in the 1950s when long-playing records had become a fact of life, no longer a novelty, my father decided to part with an immense collection of 78s and begin a new one. I was given the task of cataloguing about 3,000 records. As things turned out it seemed to be a waste of effort, because the owner of the gramophone exchange near Cambridge Circus simply measured them in bulk and offered us twelve LPs in return. But it was not entirely wasted because in the process of cataloguing I made an interesting discovery.

The record label said 'Workers' Music Association'. The band was the sort of ensemble which in even more distant times could be heard on *Workers' Playtime*: violin, saxophone, piano, bass and drums. It was a marching song. The refrain was 'And a new world will be born'. The singer was Michael Redgrave.

My father had a fine light baritone and he sang this very rum-te-tum, off-the-peg song with great feeling. The lyric made one smile condescendingly, but the emotion which his singing invested in it sounded not only authentic but stirring. I played it to my mother.

'Oh, don't!' she begged. 'Don't remind me of that dreadful thing.' She was laughing, but she was serious too.

She had been playing principal boy at the time that song was recorded, she told me, in the Unity Theatre production of *Jack and the Beanstalk*, which was the Communist Party's

59

Christmas pantomime for 1940. She described the whole experience as though she had been kidnapped, or had been sleepwalking. The giant wore a top hat, representing Capital, and rubbed his tummy. Rachel as Jack wore tights and slapped her thighs . . . She shuddered: 'Don't play it when your father's about. He hates to think about it.'

I had the satisfying feeling that I had unearthed a family skeleton, and promised myself some fun in the future. I put the record away in a safe place and that was the last I saw of it. Such is the fate of all things put in safe places. I would give a great deal for it now.

Having lost it I never had the chance to test my father's reaction to it. The opportunity passed, or more likely I simply forbore to ask what it represented and why it embarrassed him. It floated, yet another half-submerged log, one of those many topics which were seldom referred to and certainly never discussed in our everyday discourse. And even in the three years which we spent writing his autobiography, when one or two skeletons briefly rattled their bones before retiring drily and discreetly to the cupboard, it remained somewhat mysterious.

My father's introduction to politics as a young man was unusual. He started, so to say, at the top, befriended at sixteen by the son of the Prime Minister. Oliver Baldwin was gay, or rather, like my father, bisexual. He was twenty-five when Michael met him on holiday at Veules-les-Roses; he was accompanied by a friend, Johnny Boyle, and a young man called Sidney. They must have made an interesting trio: Oliver tall, with straight reddish-gold hair, piercing blue eyes, a trim officer's moustache, and the kind of masculine beauty one might find in a Pre-Raphaelite painting; Johnny Boyle florid, high-complexioned, about the same age as Oliver; and Sidney, younger, with close-cropped flaming orange hair and brightly painted face – 'the painted lady of Sidmouth', he called himself. Michael found Oliver irresistibly attractive, and I suppose that Oliver liked him well enough, although I guess from what followed that he never actually made a pass at him.

They met again in September 1926, the year Michael left Clifton College. He went to stay with Oliver at Shirburn, in the little farm cottage he shared with Johnny Boyle on the estate of Shirburn Castle. His diary describes Johnny as an 'Uranian', a term never used nowadays so far as I know, though it must have been fairly common then if Michael was familiar with it.

Monday 20th September. This morning Oliver and I had a long talk about many things. A talk such as I have not had since the old days with RJP [his first love at Clifton]. In the evening we went to Chequers to dine. I was very thrilled. It is a beautiful place with rooms too good to be out of film land.

Mrs Graham is a sweet lady, she is the caretaker there. After dinner we sat in the beautiful oak-panelled smoking room with its high windows and rich red damask curtains, its shaded lights, its gallery and old pictures.

I played and we sung. I performed 'Zucking zyder thru' a straw' with great effect.

As we drove through the long dark drive hundreds of rabbits ran across the front of the car.

The 'many things' they talked about included socialism. Oliver asked Michael to come with him to Dudley, where he had stood unsuccessfully as Labour candidate in the 1924 election and where he was to win the seat for Labour in 1929. There he would show him the living conditions, the grinding poverty in which most workers lived. He would prove to him that Britain was still two nations, and that the only hope for the great majority was socialism.

Oliver Baldwin was a pacifist and a left-wing member of the Labour Party. Neither role recommended him to the Labour Party leaders, and neither of the Labour administrations in which he served, Ramsay MacDonald's in 1929–31 and Attlee's in 1945–51, gave him promotion. Attlee's government in fact pensioned him off to what must, even then, have been an obscure fate, as Governor and Commander-in-Chief of the Leeward Islands in 1947. *Who's Who* for 1951–60 charmingly records his education as 'in football at Eton; in other things, beginning to learn'. It also records several books, a marriage in 1936 and his death in 1958. As a career, you would say, especially when compared with his illustrious father's, three times Prime Minister, this was not so distinguished. But for my father in the summer of 1926, the year of the General Strike, when Britain came closer to revolution than ever before or since, Oliver Baldwin blazed like a comet. 'From that day I could not politically call myself anything but a socialist.'

Calling himself a socialist was evidently an important step; but for the time being it did no more than help him to describe himself to himself. I do not know that he shared it with anyone else. He took no part in politics at university, though he made friends with some who did – like Guy Burgess, who designed the sets for his 1931 production of Shaw's *Captain Brassbound's Conversion* for the Cambridge Amateur Dramatic Club, and whose friendship he repaid many years later in Moscow.

The story has been vividly told by Alan Bennett in his play *An Englishman Abroad*. My father and Coral Browne were leading the Shakespeare Memorial Theatre Company on a tour to Moscow and Leningrad in 1958. It was the first tour by a British company since the war. My father was playing Hamlet.

One night after the show a very drunken Guy Burgess knocked on his dressing-room door, and invited him to lunch the next day. Then began a series of sometimes sad, sometimes absurdly funny, encounters which ended with Coral and my father taking a huge shopping list back to London for all the things Burgess missed and couldn't get in Moscow – chiefly clothes, and some old-fashioned delicacies like anchovy paste.

It was not until his thirtieth year, in 1937, that my father was moved to declare himself publicly a socialist. Then, having arrived late, he seemed determined to make up for lost time.

'I am a red-hot socialist,' he told the *Liverpool Echo*. By this time he had left the Liverpool Playhouse, as one of its brightest stars, and was playing in London at the Old Vic. 'I believe in everything to do with socialism.'

It was not such an unusual thing for a leading actor to say then, though it would be now. His friends were dying in Spain. His girlfriend at Cambridge, Mary Coss, an American student to whom he was briefly engaged, had gone back to America to join the Communist Party and was selling their paper on street corners. It was a time, as Anthony Blunt said, when all the best men were Marxists. (No they weren't, retorts Lord Annan, writing about the Cambridge spies in a recent review. 'The Marxists simply made more noise.' But yes they were, and even Lord Annan, if he had thought himself a socialist then, would probably also have thought himself a Marxist.) So, it was nothing unusual; but that interview is still very moving to read now, for me at any rate, and all the more so because in politics my father was not remotely an intellectual. He embraced socialism wholeheartedly, trustingly, and in almost the same uncomplicated way as a worker who is not easily convinced, but having been convinced commits himself totally. If it had been otherwise he might have avoided the trouble which was to follow.

'The People's Convention for a People's Covenant' was published in the Communist Party's *Daily Worker* on 28 September 1940. There had been bombing raids every night for almost eight weeks. Rachel, Vanessa and I had gone to Herefordshire to stay with Rachel's cousin Lucy. Michael had taken us to Paddington Station, where we waited on a crowded platform for about an hour and a half while several trains went out, and wondered what would happen beneath that great glass roof if an air-raid warning started.

One of the demands of the People's Convention programme was for deep bomb-proof shelters, because at that time there were none, and a very popular demand it proved to be. Working-class people living in terraced houses near to docks or factories were much the worst hit by these early raids. In the dock areas of Liverpool, for instance, the raids in that Indian summer of 1940 were so fierce that hundreds of families took their bedding and spent their nights in the open air in parks to escape the horrors of being buried or burnt alive. Little attempt had been made by the government to provide adequate protection against air raids. In London it took a big popular outcry to move the government into allowing people to take shelter in the Underground stations.

The six demands of the People's Convention programme were:

1 Defence of the people's living standards.
2 Defence of the people's democratic and trade-union rights.
3 Adequate air-raid precaution, deep bomb-proof shelters, rehousing and relief of victims.
4 Friendship with the Soviet Union.
5 A people's government, truly representative of the whole people and able to inspire the confidence of the working people of the world.
6 A people's peace that gets rid of the causes of war.

Two further demands were added later: nationalisation of the banks and basic industries, and national independence for India.

Michael was sent the programme in the form of a petition. He thought it 'a good socialist document' and signed. He was filming at the time, making *Kipps*, the third of three films he made with the director Carol Reed, and his name must have greatly helped the Communist Party's campaign, encouraging many others to sign the petition.

In February 1941 he was about to begin shooting another film, *Atlantic Ferry*, when he received a call from the BBC, asking him to come to Bentinck House for an interview. He knew what it would be about, because a composer called Lew Stone, also a signatory, had already been summoned. As he records in his diary, he was met by a Mr Streeton and another BBC official, probably a lawyer, my father thought.

They said that the Governors had decided that the People's Convention was not in the national interest, and would like to know where I stood regarding it; that I need not answer at once, could have time, etc. I replied that I didn't need time. I took the view that since the People's Convention has not been suppressed by the Government, but is a perfectly legal, constitutional method for the people of England to express themselves, it was not for the BBC to censor it, or punish its supporters. The official thanked me for making my position so clear.

I said, 'I take it that, that being the case, you do not wish to use me as a broadcaster?'

'Yes.'

'And how does that affect my contract next Sunday to sing?'

'Oh! We weren't aware that you had an outstanding contract. But that will be *quite* all right, Mr Redgrave.'

We shook hands very amicably and I was seen to the lift.

As he descended to the lift and walked away from Bentinck House he had a moment or two of regret that he had made the going so easy for them, 'and as usual a crowd of things came into my head that I might have said. But perhaps it was best so.'

It is shocking even now to read his description of this episode – shocking, even though I was myself blacklisted by the BBC for almost twenty-five years, until the autumn of 1994, because of my political activities. And what makes it especially shocking I think is that my father, the victim, was told face to face what was to happen to him. This alone makes his case unique.

The whole thing is so macabre, so utterly British. There is their invitation to go away and think the whole thing over; the politeness – 'the Governors ... would like to know where I stood'; the decency – 'We shook hands very amicably and I was seen to the lift'; and from my father a kind of weary resignation – 'But perhaps it was best so.'

Mr Streeton and the other official place the ban delicately but firmly in the context of national security – 'The Governors have decided that the People's Convention is not in the national interest' – but it must have been clear to all concerned that this was a political, not a security question. Was it legal? The decision not to enforce the ban until after the date of my father's existing contract sounds invincibly British and good-chappish but was probably guided by legal considerations. Otherwise a case could have been made for breach of contract, though only a very foolhardy person, one supposes, would have sued the BBC in those circumstances.

Sure enough, my father fulfilled his contract. He sang two songs the following Sunday, 2 March 1941, in a broadcast from the Scala Theatre: 'Smile from a Stranger' by Berkeley Fase, and Macheath's solo 'If the Heart of a Man' from *The Beggar's Opera*. The compère was called Brian Michie, and the bandleader was Debroy Somers. I don't know who else was on the bill, and I wonder if any of his fellow artistes that evening realised that this was likely to be my father's last broadcast for the BBC.

Certainly neither the studio audience nor the hundreds of thousands of listeners realised his predicament because the BBC's ban had not been reported in any newspaper. Not until 4 March, a week after the interview at Bentinck House, was news of the ban published, and then only in the *News Chronicle*, which made it their top story, with a picture of my father, alongside the main war news, Molotov's warning to Bulgaria. The *Daily Telegraph* had telephoned his home in the small hours, just after midnight, asking for confirmation of the *News Chronicle* story, which by then had appeared in the first edition. But the *Telegraph* decided not to report it.

The following day the *News Chronicle* again put the story on the front page, with a picture of my mother attending a protest meeting organised by the Workers' Music Association. They reported that the National Council for Civil Liberties had protested against the ban, and would itself be holding a meeting at Conway Hall in Red Lion Square. But again no other newspaper mentioned the story. This was strange indeed, especially given that the *Daily Express* had weeks before published an attack by their columnist Jonah Barrington, in which he had questioned the patriotism and the motives of those who supported the People's Convention, and had wondered aloud why a national organisation like the BBC was giving them employment.

Pressure was mounting on my father. His agent, Jack Dunfee, telephoned to say that Ted Black and Maurice Ostrer, the producers of *Atlantic Ferry* and two of the most powerful men in the British film industry, were 'wild with rage' and wanted to meet him in Dunfee's apartment in Claridges. They wanted Michael to hold a conference and tell the press that he would be joining the navy in June. Above all they wanted him to withdraw his support from the People's Convention. My father told them that he knew what he was doing and had no intention of withdrawing his signature. He offered to hand back the contract for his next film, *Jeannie*.

Yet he was becoming increasingly confused. The 'good socialist document' which he had signed in late autumn 1940, with its six demands, looked more and more ambiguous under the glare of the publicity to which it was now subjected. For instance, it had demanded 'a people's peace'. Some 23,000 civilians had been killed in air raids by the end of 1940, and more than 50,000 wounded. In areas like Stepney in the East End of London whole streets had been demolished, and towns the size of Plymouth and Coventry had been almost flattened. With whom would a 'people's government' sign a treaty for a 'people's peace'? With Hitler?

His friends told him that he was naïve, that he was being 'used', and he began to feel that he was. He was told that the People's Convention was a front organisation for the Communist Party, which had been banned, and its paper the *Daily Worker* suppressed, in January 1941. That was not perhaps so surprising or disturbing because he was well aware that many of its leading members and most of its organisers and activists were members of the CP. The problem went deeper, to the whole policy of the CP itself.

Very few people remember this period in the history of the Communist Party of Great Britain. Until August 1939 the party had been calling for a defensive alliance between Britain and the USSR against Hitler. Most of the support which the party had won reflected the growing fear and hatred of fascism. For several days after the signing of the Molotov–Ribbentrop pact the *Daily Worker* continued its calls for all-out struggle against the Nazis. But then Dave Springhall, the party's representative in Moscow, returned to London with instructions that the party must change its line: they must show that it was Britain and France which had declared war and were the aggressors. They must cease their primitive chorus of anti-fascism and argue that the war was an imperialist war, especially on Britain's part. In short, they must campaign for peace. As the manifesto of the Central Committee put it: 'The people must take a hand. The immediate issue is the ending of hostilities and the calling of a peace conference.'

Even the British Communist Party Central Committee, which of all CPs was notoriously the most ready to accommodate itself to any shift of policy and every accompanying order from Moscow, had difficulties adjusting to this new line. When, thanks to the changes ushered in by perestroika, the minutes of the meeting at which these orders were discussed were finally published for the first time in 1989, they showed Harry Pollitt arguing vehemently against, and then resigning as General Secretary of the Communist Party.

At the height of the furore in March 1941, the CP issued a statement: 'The People's Convention is not a "stop the war" movement. It is not a movement for "peace at any price". It is irreconcilably opposed to Fascism or to any victory of Fascism.' Almost every word of this is an evasion. Many of the Convention's supporters, including Michael, were indeed opposed to fascism. However, the reason why they now had to be defended against the charge that they considered the victory of fascism to be the lesser evil was the fact that the CP, from September 1939 until 22 June 1941 when the USSR was invaded, was absolutely opposed, on orders from Moscow, to any pursuit of victory *against* fascism.

'What is our attitude to the possibility of defeat? What

should we do in the event that Germany invades Britain?' Such were the questions he found himself asking his friends in the CP. But he got only evasive or cynical answers. 'What about those who say that the CP is only using the Convention and will drop it the moment it suits it to do so?' he asked one friend, Geoffrey Parsons. It was a very pertinent question indeed, considering that that was exactly what happened after the Nazi invasion of the USSR. 'So what?' was the reply. He mentioned this question and Parson's reply to D. N. Pritt, but Pritt only compounded his confusion.

A meeting with Pritt had been arranged at the latter's suggestion, though not only on his initiative. The CP must have realised that my father was likely to withdraw his support, and were trying to stiffen his resolve. First they sent the great scientist J. B. S. Haldane to have a chat with him one afternoon at the film studios. Then came the meeting with Pritt, at his country house.

D. N. Pritt was a successful barrister, a King's Counsel, well known as a friend of the Communist Party and a publicist for Stalin's system in the Soviet Union. He had reported the 1930s Moscow trials for the Labour weekly *New Statesman*, and his enthusiastic endorsement of the show trials as examples of a new and higher kind of socialist justice undoubtedly helped the CP to face down any doubters in its own ranks and shout down any opposition from outside.

Pritt was charming, relaxed, urbane. He met Michael at Reading station in a chauffeur-driven Bentley. They had lunch in his dining-room overlooking the river, decorated with plates with Soviet motifs from the old imperial potteries, and after lunch they walked many times round his beautiful garden. The Dean of Canterbury (Dr Hewlett-Johnson, later known as the 'Red Dean') had also had his doubts, but was now convinced and was still 'staunch'. Probably, when all this had 'blown over', Pritt joked, Michael would be awarded the Order of Lenin. (That was clever. Michael naïvely supposed that he meant it seriously, and immediately felt guilty, because there was no honour he would have felt happier to receive.)

'Keep your head down. It'll blow over,' was the extent of Pritt's wisdom. And, ironically, up to a point it did. On 20 March, Churchill made a statement to the House of Commons informing them that the BBC was going to lift its ban.

It would be comforting to think that the BBC had bowed to the pressure of public opinion. Twelve artists had been banned for supporting the People's Convention, including the composer Alan Bush. Some very popular artists spoke out against the ban and demanded that it be lifted. Leslie Howard organised a petition from all the actors working at Denham Film Studios. Laurence Olivier telephoned, most indignant, saying, 'I thought this was the kind of thing we were supposed to be fighting against.'

At first the BBC was unmoved. 'The policy of the BBC is not to invite any person to the microphone whose views are opposed to the war effort.' But the protest grew. Harold Laski and forty Labour MPs circulated a letter against the ban. Vaughan Williams withdrew permission for the BBC to broadcast his latest work. E. M. Forster headed the platform of speakers at the meeting organised by the National Council for Civil Liberties at Conway Hall. He told the audience that he would not fulfil two contracts for talks with the BBC until the ban was lifted. Other speakers included the Dean of Westminster, Beatrix Lehmann, Philip Cardew and my father.

Certainly these protests were a decisive factor, but I am also sure that the government realised that a mistake had been made, and that they must correct it by making the BBC lift the ban. It was as important to the government to preserve the appearance of the fairness and independence of the BBC as it was necessary that the true content of that appearance should be the total subordination of the BBC to the government's policy.

As recently as 1977, a former director-general of the BBC, Sir Hugh Greene, could say that 'one thing I can state quite categorically is that there has never been any victimisation of anyone for their political views at the BBC.' Greene may have believed that to be true, but he could only have done so by turning a blind eye to practices that had existed at the BBC since 1937, practices that would continue at least until 1985 and almost certainly up to the present day. Some details of the BBC's blacklisting of staff and artists were published by the *Observer* in 1985. On the first floor of Broadcasting House, in those very corridors which Orwell used as his model for the Ministry of Truth, was Room 105: the office, they said, of Brigadier Ronald Stonham. Stonham's official description was 'special assistant' to the Director of Personnel. What this meant was that he was the BBC's liaison officer with MI5, for the purpose of vetting and blacklisting.

When this was published the BBC admitted that certain staff appointments were subject to vetting for security, but claimed that the procedures were entirely under their control. 'Only the BBC decides who to appoint to any post within the Corporation. No external agency has the right to veto the appointment or promotion of any member of the staff,' they said.

The government, of course, defended the practice. Giles Shaw, then the Home Office Minister of State, said: 'The government believes, as have successive governments over a long period, that it is in the national interest for the BBC to apply certain necessary security procedures.'

He was right to say that this had happened 'over a long period'. The practice of vetting was established by the BBC's founder Sir John Reith. He was a member of a sub-committee of the Committee of Imperial Defence which decided, in 1935, that 'in time of war or when the threat of an emergency was imminent, the government should assume effective control over broadcasting and the BBC.' In 1937 the Ullswater Committee on the future of broadcasting recommended that 'in serious or national emergencies, the government control over the BBC would be necessary.' Reith's diaries record that on 5 March 1937 he saw the Home Secretary, Sir John Simon, to negotiate a contract between the BBC and the government 'in case of war'. The terms of that contract were not made public, but it seems more than likely that they would have included a system of security vetting.

That this system extended not only to staff but to performers, writers and composers can be seen from Michael's experience. That it existed not only in wartime, when the appeal to 'national interest' would seem to be more persuasive, but in conditions which could never be considered as 'national emergency' is of course much harder to prove, though some thorough research by the *Guardian* journalist Richard Norton-Taylor and Mark Hollingsworth in their book *Blacklist* goes a long way to proving it.

What was exceptional about the banning of Michael Redgrave and the supporters of the People's Convention was that it was made public. The evidence suggests that neither the BBC nor the government wanted it to be. Mr Streeton and the BBC official may have felt they could count on my father and others not to seek publicity for the fact that they had been banned, especially since, in Michael's case at least, this would be likely to have serious consequences in other kinds of employment, for instance in films. No newspaper reported the ban until a week after Michael had been told of it. And when it was finally reported by the *News Chronicle* no other newspaper published the story for two days, which suggests that some form of D-notice, however ineffective, was in operation. Hulton's leader in *Picture Post*, 'Let There be Freedom', came much later, in fact within a day of the announcement that the ban was to be lifted. It was full of nauseating sentiment, and many patronising references to my father, but it makes the case, which was surely uppermost in the government's thinking if not in the BBC's, that the BBC must be seen to be fair as well as independent, in contrast to the propaganda systems of Britain's enemies.

Three days after the ban was lifted, on 23 March, Michael wrote to Pritt asking that his name be removed from the list of supporters of the People's Convention. Three months later his call-up papers arrived and he joined the Royal Navy. By then Germany had invaded Russia. This time the Communist Party had no difficulty in changing their political line, literally overnight. The war which for nearly two years had been an imperialist war, in which Britain had been the aggressor, now became the Great Patriotic War, and the CP transformed itself from an opponent of the war to its most fervent recruiting sergeant.

No discernible damage was done to my father's career as an actor; but damage of a subtle kind was done, and was far harder to undo.

7

Politics in Time of War

ℚ

My father began his basic naval training at HMS *Drake*, in Devonport, on 30 June 1941. He was thirty-three years old, married with two children; the third, Lynn, was conceived a year later. The photograph of his class shows him seated in the front row, smiling from ear to ear. He is head and shoulders taller than all the other ratings. Average height for men was only 5 feet 7½ inches and would not increase markedly until the improved diet of children during the war and in the postwar years began to have effect. But it is not only in height that he seems to stand out from the rest. Even a less partial eye than mine, if it looked along these rows of smiling, good-natured, knobbly faces, might come to rest on his face and see in it a focus for the group as a whole.

He chose the navy partly because my mother's father and brothers were naval and not military. Rachel's father was headmaster at the Royal Naval College at Dartmouth, and it was in the chapel of the college that Michael and Rachel were married. Of her two younger brothers the elder, Nicholas, had joined the navy as a professional sailor before the war. Robin, the younger, joined the Royal Naval Volunteer Reserve in 1939. In the summer of 1940 he was on extended sick leave suffering from shell shock. Robin was all the family's favourite, with his carrotty-red hair, open friendly face and loud hearty laugh. He declared himself fit and returned to active service, and his ship the *Prince of Wales* was torpedoed in the disastrous action off

74

Singapore. In the evacuation from Malaya in 1942 his tugboat was fired on. He was last seen swimming, but he had a dislocated arm and typically had given his lifebelt to a shipmate.

Michael never saw any action. For a month or so in the autumn he went to sea in the battleship *Illustrious*, but only for trials off the coast of Norfolk, Virginia, where the ship had been refitted. He had applied for a commission but was still an ordinary seaman, and while he was ammunitioning one of the *Illustrious*'s guns he injured an arm so that after a spell of treatment back home in Liverpool the Admiralty decided to release him, back to civilian life and the theatre.

The men he describes below decks in his letters to my mother are the sort you will meet any day still in a National Health Service hospital or a prison waiting-room, or at a football match, or an English seaside resort – the only difference being that there are no Asian or Afro-Caribbean faces in Michael's class of '41. They are tolerant and immensely friendly. ('The friendliness is indescribable, it could make anything bearable.') They carry on with their amusements whenever they can as if war and its destruction were just a nuisance. ('Plymouth is almost entirely flat. But, incredibly, there are still people about, and singing in the pubs, and bathing at the Hoe, and in the evenings dancing on the Hoe.') They swear a great deal. They are hardly at all religious, and not much interested in politics. They grumble incessantly but put up with great discomfort and sometimes terrible pain with extraordinary stoicism. They don't care for snobbery, of which, even in the navy with its supposedly more democratic traditions, there is still plenty. ('Didn't tell you of my interview last Friday, with the Divisional Commander. Jeremy Hutchinson, Peggy Ashcroft's husband. He told me he was going to relieve me of being class leader, because Menzies had to be tried. He said, "I'm thoroughly satisfied with your performance, and have put you down as commission-worthy. It's just that Menzies, do you see, is secretary to the Duke of Atholl and we have had a little pressure!"')

What are they fighting against? Against Hitler, it seems,

which is not quite the same as saying against fascism. Or rather Hitler personifies fascism, and is also personally responsible for air raids, shortages and especially for the fact that they have had to interrupt their lives and put on uniform. What are they fighting for? That is harder to answer, because there is no one as yet to articulate what they want. Sir William Beveridge has yet to make his entrance. Beveridge, 'the People's William', must rank as one of the most unlikely figures ever to articulate the mood of the masses, but that, in his dry prissy tones, he undoubtedly did. His report, published a few days after the victory at Alamein, sold 100,000 copies in a few weeks, and 685,000 in all. Nineteen out of twenty men and women in the armed forces knew and understood its principles, even though by the end of 1942 the Army Information Bureau refused to circulate them.

Beveridge's report and its immense success helps one to understand the popularity of the People's Convention, which impressed even George Orwell, who loathed it so much that he physically tore down its posters.

22nd January [1941]
— is convinced, perhaps rightly, that the danger of the People's Convention racket is much under-estimated and that one must fight back and not ignore it. He says that thousands of simple-minded people are taken in by the appealing programme of the People's Convention and do not realize that it is a defeatist manoeuvre intended to help Hitler. He quoted a letter from the Dean of Canterbury who said 'I want you to understand that I am whole-heartedly for winning the war, and that I believe Winston Churchill to be the only possible leader for us till the war is over' (or words to that effect), and nevertheless supported the People's Convention. It appears that there are thousands like this.*

Until Beveridge there was a vacuum in politics in which there was no official expression of Britain's war aims, no party

---

* George Orwell, 'Wartime Diary: 1941', from *The Collected Essays, Journalism and Letters*, volume 2 (Penguin, 1970).

political opposition (the Labour Party leaders had entered Churchill's coalition), nor any organised expression to the government's conduct of the war. A huge gap existed between the reactionary-patriotic outlook and politics of Britain's leaders and the defeatist pro-Hitler position of a very small though still vocal minority. In that vacuum the programme of the People's Convention, despite its equivocations, could gather significant support and might have gathered considerably more if the Communist Party had not changed its tune in June 1941.

Hence the venom with which the public argument against the Convention's supporters was conducted. What amounted to a revolutionary situation existed in Britain, though there was no leader and no party to give voice to it. After twenty years of living on an appallingly inadequate diet, people suddenly woke up, in the summer of 1940, to what their leaders were and how negligently they had prepared for the war. The leaders themselves sensed this mood and were badly scared by it.

There is yet another element, however: the determination of the vast majority to resist invasion. When in the autumn of 1940 Cabinet Minister Anthony Eden appealed for a force of Local Defence Volunteers, later the Home Guard, he got a quarter of a million volunteers in the first twenty-four hours and another million in the next month. There was no mood of defeatism and little or no pacifism when it seemed that invasion was likely. However popular the rest of its programme, it was here, on the question of 'a people's peace', that the People's Convention was totally out of step with the popular mood. Michael sensed this, and though he could scarcely understand the reasons why it was so he must have felt the ground opening up beneath him. This impression emerges in his diary:

Sunday, 16 March 1941.
To Royal Hotel for Convention. 10–1, 2–6. A long, depressing day, full of disappointment and dismay. Can see very well why movement is charged with revolutionary defeatism. Everyone who speaks airs grievances. Man speaks of our intolerably inhuman

blockade! One thinks of sailors being machine-gunned. Long several times to get up and say 'But what about the war? What is our attitude towards the possibility of defeat? Why do you all cheer every time Russia is mentioned? Friendship with the USSR certainly – but England must do better than that.

Despite this whole episode, and even to some extent because of it, my father remained a very popular and respected figure. A poll in February 1943, run by all the national newspapers, still put him third in the list of most popular British actors, although no film of his had been released in the last twelve months. At the beginning of the year he was approached by Sir Richard Acland, who tried to persuade him to stand for his new party, Common Wealth, in the North Portsmouth by-election.

3 January 1943.
At 12, by appointment, Jackson, secretary of Common Wealth, came and suggested I contest the North Portsmouth constituency, vacated by Sir Roger Keyes being made a baron. Wintringham, he says, is contesting Midlothian on the same lines as Gladstone did for the Liberals! And Wintringham says I'd win 25 per cent more supporters for Common Wealth all over the country. Jackson says I'd win any election by 2–1 majority!!

Sir Richard Acland was a wealthy minor aristocrat, the fifteenth baronet. He had been a Liberal MP in 1935, but at the beginning of the war announced his conversion to socialism or, as he called it, common ownership. He published two very successful pamphlets, *Unser Kampf* and the *Manifesto of the Ordinary Man*, and formed a small movement called Forward March, which soon developed into a political party named Common Wealth. The Communist Party attacked it ferociously and claimed that it was fascist (the ban on the *Daily Worker* had been lifted), and it is not difficult to see why. Common Wealth declared themselves ready to work with any party on the political left, the sole condition being that they would break the electoral truce with the Conservatives; and this neither the

CP nor, much more importantly, the Labour Party was prepared to do. Throughout the war the Labour Party had an electoral 'pairing' arrangement whereby the party which had won the seat in the previous election would stand unopposed in by-elections. Acland's Common Wealth won three by-elections against the coalition. Their programme was similar, though to the left of, the People's Convention: nationalisation of banks, land and industry; full independence for India; and a commitment for Britain to share all her wealth and resources with poorer countries.

The success of Common Wealth in wartime by-elections was an important factor in persuading the Labour leaders (though not all, and not Attlee) to end the coalition and campaign for a Labour government in 1945. There were other portents. In a mock-parliament of soldiers serving in North Africa, Common Wealth were voted into 'government' and knocked Labour into second place. The Labour leaders reluctantly came to realise that unless they ended the coalition and put forward an independent programme Common Wealth might win a large number of seats and replace the Liberals (though well to the left of them) as the third major party. As it was, Acland and his comrades returned to the Labour Party and Common Wealth became a footnote in history, though nominally it still exists even today.

Acland told Michael he could become the most popular political leader in Britain, and incredible as that sounds today it must have seemed not at all absurd at the time. He continued to court him for a while, but Michael continued to refuse. He voted Labour in 1945, and until then he was an active leading member of Equity. But he played no part in politics. Perhaps he was right not to, though I'm certain it caused him some regret. Regret and disappointment are wonderfully conveyed in his performance as Hamer Radshaw in the 1947 film of *Fame is the Spur*. Radshaw's character was modelled, by the novelist Howard Spring, on Ramsay MacDonald. He dies of a heart attack as he struggles to unsheath a sword from its scabbard. The sword has hung over his mantelpiece for years, as a trophy or a sentimental reminder of the battle of Peterloo.

We children, growing up in Chiswick after the war in a very privileged household, with a cook, a nanny and a gardener, were unthinking flag-waving little conservatives. When my father noticed our conservatism he tried to counteract it, but feebly. He entered our nursery one morning, where the only newspaper to be seen was our nanny's *Daily Mail*, waving a copy of the *News Chronicle* at us. 'Read this for a change,' he said, in the slightly over-purposeful, too loud voice he used when he wasn't sure of his ground or felt embarrassed. Sure enough he left the room the next instant, leaving us to wonder in what respect he thought the *Chronicle* superior to the *Mail*, and with no inkling that he meant us to see that a person's choice of newspaper is a political act – in Michael's case by now the sole remaining political act.

When our politics changed in adult life he tried briefly to protest, but soon retreated behind a wall of pained silence. And there, to my lasting regret, I left him, until the very end of his life, thinking it about as pointless to discuss politics with him as he thought it would be upsetting to discuss them with me.

8

Loving Women

♋

'They like a compliment, you see.'

My father was instructing me in the facts of life – 'They' being women, or ladies, depending on the context. Women were 'women' for all everyday purposes but 'ladies' when they became the object of a man's desire, as in 'so-and-so has a new lady friend'. My father had just given me a practical demonstration.

'That's pretty, Joan.'

Joan Sparks was his new secretary. She wore a green silk scarf, 'Jacqmar' from Fenwicks in Bond Street.

'Do you think so?'

'Very pretty.'

Yes, I could see, she did like the compliment. She smiled sweetly, as if flattered and half surprised. And I felt flattered that my father had shared one of his secrets with me. I only wished he would share some more.

But such, only, were the facts of life I learned from him – of sex, or what are sometimes disparagingly called the mechanics of sex, nothing at all. If learning is the progress from ignorance to knowledge I had to crawl or stumble darkly over mountains of ignorance, illuminated only by *Health and Efficiency* or its French equivalent, *Ma Cahute au Canada*, Willard Motley's novel *Knock on Any Door*, or Alberto Moravia's *Woman of Rome*, or *100 Best Short Stories Chosen by W. Somerset Maughan*. Nothing from my father, who did not even share a risqué story with us as children, let alone a dirty joke. I of course took it for granted that my father knew all about it and would tell me in his own good time.

I grew up surrounded, as it seemed to me, by women, and all of them adored, worshipped or feared my father.

There was my elder sister Vanessa. She could always tell me things about him that I didn't know, which made me realise she must be close to him and share his secrets in a way I never could.

'What do you talk about?'

I knew she had hours-long conversations with him, because she told me so, and I begged to be included in them, no matter how indirectly.

'Everything,' she said with a triumphant smile.

It was from Vanessa, more than any other person, that I realised my father knew everything. He of course was modest and concealed the fact as best he could, but she explained that he was absolutely omniscient.

'I bet he's not. There must be some things he doesn't know,' I protested.

'Yes, you would think that,' she said.

We shared a governess, a Miss Glascot, who began to teach us French. I have never forgotten the excitement of those first steps in learning French, finding a word like *chou*, and discovering that it meant 'cabbage': 'Savez-vous planter les choux?'; 'Genou, hibou, joujou, chou . . .' But my greatest excitement was to find something I could teach my father, something he wouldn't know. When the lesson was over I tore out of the little room in the cottage which was the annexe to our house and had been turned into our schoolroom, and found my father underneath the canopy of wistaria where we had lunch in the summer. I challenged him, point-blank:

'Do you know the French for cabbage?'

'*Chou*,' he said.

I never felt smaller or more in awe of him in my life. He didn't have to pause for thought or search his memory; it came out just like that, on demand, from the infinite storehouse of his knowledge.

'That's right,' I said.

'What else did you learn?' he asked.

'*Genou, hibou, joujou* – do you know what those mean?'

'Yes.'

I walked away. Learning would never be so sweet again, because whatever I learned I would only be catching up with what he already knew. Suddenly a vast interminable landscape was spread out in front of me, morning after morning; get up, go to school, do your homework, go to bed, get up again and repeat the whole dreary process, and beyond Miss Glascot would be prep school, and beyond prep school would be Westminster, and beyond Westminster would be . . . And at the end of all this would I have caught up with him? No; because, as Vanessa also told me, although grown up he was still learning things.

'What things?'

'About the fourth dimension.'

'What's that?'

'We don't know whether it exists. We think it does.'

So that was it. I was seven years old and I was totally depressed, because I realised that morning that even if this year I caught up halfway with my father, and next year another half, I would never close the gap completely.

Another woman who adored my father was his first secretary, Edith Hargraves. She had worked in a bank as a young woman until she inherited some money, enough to give her independence and to indulge her two passions, theatre and cricket. She would follow England's cricketers to the ends of the earth, and in the summer months she went to Lord's every day to watch Middlesex. It was the heyday of Compton and Edrich, and Denis Compton was my idol. Edith would collect me in the morning during the holidays, and we would spend the rest of the day in the Lord's grandstand. I soon realised that she knew nothing at all about the finer points of cricket, not even elementary field placings like square leg or cover point. On the other hand she read voraciously and had a very retentive memory, and she could tell you things about Compton which not even the most goggle-eyed fan would know, like the colour of his bathroom curtains. She called him 'Denis', rarely using his surname, which she pronounced in the old-fashioned way as 'Cumpton', and talked about him with such easy affectionate familiarity that the old gentlemen round about us in the grandstand must have thought she was his mother.

'Denis'll show them,' she would say, settling back comfortably with an egg-and-cress sandwich.

It was my first ever visit to Lord's, and Somerset were playing Middlesex. Somerset batted first and Harold Gimblett, probably the best opening batsman in those days not to play for England, scored a century. But the rest of the side was skittled out by two new spin bowlers, Fred Titmus and Ian Bedford. Then at about 5.15 in the afternoon sunshine it was Middlesex's turn. Jack Robertson was soon back in the pavilion and in came Edrich – 'Bill', as Edith called him. But even 'Bill' looked unsteady against Somerset's pace bowlers.

'He'll get better when Denis comes in,' Edith explained. 'Denis brings out the best in him. The terrible twins.' She laughed.

As if on cue another wicket fell, and Denis Compton sauntered out to the wicket.

'Does he really use Brylcream?' You could ask Edith questions like that.

'Oh yes. And he keeps a little comb in his pocket, very small. You'll see. Watch him when he passes his hand over his head, like this' – she demonstrated – 'he's really combing his hair. You watch.'

Compton fully justified her faith and mine that evening. With only twenty minutes left on the clock, when any other batsman would have played safe to come back next morning, Compton tore into Somerset's attack, pulling it, cutting it and driving it with the kind of recklessness which made us love him.

Her other passion was theatre, and next to theatre ballet. She was on first-name terms with all the leading actors and dancers of the day, but though she loved them all equally and quite uncritically she adored my father.

She had been Edith Evans's secretary and that was how she came to be secretary to Michael. But she adored him so totally that she could not bear to bring him bad news, or even let him glance at it. Bills and all distasteful things like income tax demands she simply buried out of sight. 'My Mikey doesn't want to know about income tax,' she would say, and whether he did or didn't she simply hid all demands from him, paying what she could and stalling what she couldn't until a time came when the inspectors could be stalled no more. Disaster followed: bailiffs, and then bankruptcy courts, from which he was rescued by his agent – but at a price. He had to agree to do whatever work his agent put in front of him, on whatever terms, for the next two years. My father suffered. He had always prided himself that he only took on work he had chosen to do, and now he could no longer make that boast. Yet no one it seemed could bring themselves to blame Edith for the disaster, because everything she did was done from pure love. My mother blamed her a little, it is true. She found Edith's adoration quite hard to take at the best of times, and especially when it entailed such dreadful consequences.

'Oh God,' my mother would say, 'there's Edith again. Wouldn't you know?'

If you went to see my father in any performance from 1942 until 1979 you would be likely to have seen Edith in the audience. You would have heard her, too, because she had a louder and more distinctive voice than any of the actors – unmusical as a corncrake, oblivious of distance, time or place, announcing that yes, this would be the nineteenth time she had seen him in the role.

Edith was as much without discrimination where my father was concerned as she was innocent of any reason why Compton might pad up defensively to one ball and then open his shoul-

ders to hit the next ball out of the ground. It was of no interest
to her to judge whether the nineteenth performance was better
than the first, or even different: they were all 'marvellous'.

My father had a large number of fans who followed him
from theatre to theatre. Some were mad, like the woman who
cried out that he had married her in Glasgow. One was danger-
ous, they said, and had to be taken away in an ambulance.
Most of them, however, were no more than mildly dotty, and
some, like Edith, were in all other respects normal. There was
never any competition between them, nor any ill will. But Edith
unquestionably was supreme.

In medieval monasteries there used to be a place for men
and women who were not quite holy enough to be monks
or nuns but were sufficiently devout to live next door to the
monastery and have some nominal occupation such as keeper
of the keys. No doubt in heaven or hell or wherever one might
find my father in the fourth dimension one would find Edith
in the anteroom.

Then there was our nanny, Kathleen or 'Kitty' Randall. She
arrived when I was three and stayed until I was twenty-one
and in my last year at university. She had gone to work at
fifteen as a nursery maid in a house in Norfolk; by the time
she reached us at Bromyard in Herefordshire she was fifty and
had a lifetime's work behind her, the kind of strenuously hard
work which leaves its marks on a body. Her hands were gnarled
and cracked from washing and scrubbing, and in the cold
weather the cracks would open and make her sing with pain.
Her feet went better after a visit to the chiropodist, except
when he was drunk and cut off the end of her big toe, but on
most days she was lame from climbing, morning, noon and
night, from cellar to attic, in the big houses she had worked
in.

Yet she was unique. Alone among all the women around me
she obviously did not adore my father, and though she was
too professional a person to allow her disapproval to be obvious she showed it in plenty of small ways. She was at war with

anything she considered pretentious, and with anyone who gave themselves 'airs and graces'. It was a crusade, her war against gentility, and many who came into our household, including Edith, fell foul of it. 'Lady Muck!' she would explode, as Edith left the room, though always *sotto voce* and after she had closed the door. My father was neither pretentious nor genteel, but she treated him as if he were because his personality was altogether too unpredictable for her liking.

It was impossible altogether to ignore her disapproval, for she showed it so clearly, like an old soldier's over-elaborate salute to an incompetent officer. But as I partly understood and partly disapproved myself I never commented upon it. One reason was the fact that my father neglected my younger sister Lynn.

Lynn was born on 8 March 1943. I would have said that her birth was an anticlimax, except that an anticlimax requires some prior sense of expectation or excitement, and there is simply no mention of Rachel's pregnancy in the months before. The event itself is noted, but that is all.

> Our second daughter was born about 8.15. Sleeping at the Meurice when Dr Lew telephoned. Phoned Andy, Margaret, Eric, Adrianne, Noel. Up and to Franklin's for ring and to Fortnum's for flowers. To Clinic. 'Lynn' very podgy, with blue hands, blowing bubbles. R well and had a comparatively good time of it.

What a far cry it seems from my own birth, four years before, when my father filled three pages in his diary, describing each moment of his pacing up and down in the room below. What a contrast even with the gaiety of Lynn's conception nine months earlier: 'To Quaglinos with Rachel. Lovely white burgundy and the day ends triumphantly!' (This was written on 7 June 1942, so one assumes it may have been the evening of Lynn's conception.)

When the rocket attacks began we children went back to Bromyard. My parents stayed in London, acting together in *Uncle Harry* at the Garrick Theatre. Our nanny looked after us in a little cottage in Bromyard village, lent by an aunt of Rachel's. By the time we returned to London, to a flat in River-mead Court in Putney, nearly two years had passed. My father must have seemed a stranger to Lynn, and she was perhaps frightened or shy of him. At all events my father, who never liked to enter a race unless he had decided to win it, seemed to give up the challenge of winning her affection.

There was another reason for nanny's disapproval. My father, at about this time or soon after we returned to London, no longer shared my mother's bed. I doubt if nanny knew the reason for this; but she knew something was amiss and she disapproved of it.

And of course there was my mother. But she must have a space of her own, and does not exactly belong here – not yet – where everyone except Vanessa seemed to be a kind of substitute for my mother.

'Too low! Too low!'

My father was a poor sleeper, an insomniac. To compensate for his wretched nights he slept late into the morning, or tried to. We lived at Bedford House in Chiswick Mall, where the road runs past the houses and beyond the road runs the river Thames. It is a very quiet road, with few cars and no traffic; but to an insomniac like my father the mew of a seagull was a deafening racket. A passing tug or an aeroplane would bring him to his bedroom window roaring with anger.

'Too low! Too low!' he would yell, at the full stretch of his lungs, at some distant speck of a passing aeroplane on its way to Heathrow. It was half past eleven in the morning, when the rest of the household had long since been up and was tiptoeing about its business, but it was understood that my father must not be disturbed. Understood by everyone except me: I thought it one of the many ways in which my father was over-indulged.

'What *was* that noise?' my mother would ask, knowing perfectly well the answer. She loved my father's heavy operatic jokes, and would be sure to tell us later how he had shouted at an aeroplane.

By now it would be quarter to twelve and time to find out whether he wanted lunch, and if so what he wanted and when he wanted it. By a quarter past twelve he might have completed the business of getting up, and would set off for a walk along the river or in Chiswick Park, stopping off at the Feathers on the way back for a cider. Then lunch, followed by another hour or so of rest during which we had to creep about like ghosts, because if he were woken he would roar like a bison.

It was not that he was lazy. He worked, at this time of his life, prodigiously hard. But they were his hours, his timetable and his household, and if he was selfish it was the selfishness of genius. That was how my mother arranged it. She loved us all as children, equally and devotedly. But she too adored and worshipped my father in ways which I could only marvel at.

9

Loving Men

☺

Biography is a kind of revenge. Why must I take revenge? For all the things my father never told me? For all the secrets he kept from me? For all the life he lived without me? Or just for having died?

Or is it like pressing my face against the railings of the school playground watching my son at play? He is quite oblivious of my presence watching him. He is wearing the clothes I put on him this morning, but he wears them somehow differently. I can see him trying to make friends with a bigger boy who just ignores him. I see him being pushed or falling over and I want to intervene. But the playground is for learning about life, and I mustn't intervene because it won't help him. 'He has to fight his own battles.'

Only now it is my father I am watching. And he is oblivious of me, of course, reading his diaries, leafing through his letters, peering at this and that, the little half-truths, the fears, the anxieties he tried to conceal. This is his private face, the face he didn't want to show to the world. Of course, I say to myself, I am trying to show the whole man, trying to know him better. Yet the better I know him the stranger he becomes to me.

Of course there are familiar landmarks, like his wedding. Familiar because I have heard about it many times and I feel as if I was there, a member of his wedding. Familiar things like the crack in the paving stone between the garden gate and the front door. It has always been there and it always will and I don't have to do anything about it. These are the stories that are so familiar that when my mother tells them I can prompt her if she forgets a name or a detail.

My parents' wedding. My father looks proud in his penguin suit. He smiles with his lips closed because he is shy about his teeth. He hasn't yet learned to smile like a film star, with his teeth bared, and won't need to learn for a few years yet. Even in *The Lady Vanishes* he still smiles with closed lips. My mother looks as if she is about to faint.

It all happened so quickly.

'Tuesday 12 March 1935. Rehearse Act II *Flowers of the Forest*,' my father wrote, recording the new production at Liverpool. 'Rachel Kempson is Naomi. Taller than I had feared. To lunch with her, Bon Marché.'

Rachel was 5 feet 8 inches tall, but my father had seen her play Hero in *Much Ado About Nothing* the year before at Stratford, and for some reason had got the impression that she was tiny. 'Taller than I had feared' is such a strange, grudging, nothing sort of a compliment. 'Lunch with her, Bon Marché' is a good beginning, though.

Two weeks later they seem to be no further forward, though the proprietor of the Bon Marché may have raised an eyebrow. But then the show opens and suddenly – there is no other way to describe it – fate intervenes.

Word rehearsal. Lunch Bon Marché Rachel. Haircut – not successful. Home. Change. First performance *Flowers of the Forest*. Accident with lights. To comfort R afterwards. Extraordinary meeting. To Adelphi with Geoff, Valerie, and R. Home with R.

Thank heaven for that 'accident with lights'. It is the sort of accident which in time-travel stories plays a crucial part in the scheme of things. John Van Druten's *Flowers of the Forest* is a romantic tale. My father as Richard went to switch off the light before folding Naomi, my mother, in his arms. The electrician was dozing and missed his cue. Cursing under his breath my father took his hand off the switch to kiss my mother, and just then the electrician woke up and remembered his cue. The audience laughed and a tender romantic scene was almost ruined.

I cannot help seeing the hand of fate disguised as a sleepy electrician – especially when the next night he falls asleep again, in the same scene.

Thursday 28 March. To town. Rachel at 12 Bon Marché. Then steamer to New Brighton. Glorious sunny day. Tea. Home. Second performance. Same accident. Home with R.

After that their affair sped forward on roller skates. The next three entries in my father's diary end with the single letter 'R'. Then there is a gap of several days, with no entries. Then a single pencilled entry on Sunday 7 April, 'Became engaged to R'. Then another gap, of a week. Then on Sunday 14 April another pencilled entry, 'Eric Kempson': Rachel's father and now Michael's prospective father-in-law. Then a long gap, before Monday 15 July, 'To Dartmouth'. And then marriage on Thursday 18 July.

All this has been familiar to me for as long as I can recall, though Michael's diary in its laconic way makes it seem once more fresh and delightful. What followed was familiar also. My father had taken driving lessons so that he could drive away from the wedding reception. 'Could he drive?' we used to ask incredulously. In our household Rachel did all the driving. Michael never, ever drove, though whether on principle or simply because he couldn't we weren't sure.

As we grew up my mother added other touches to the story, and they in turn became familiar too. How she was a virgin when they were married, and very nervous. How my father was nervous also, although more experienced. She told how one afternoon in Liverpool, soon after the 'accident with the lights', when they were lying on the carpet in the sitting-room of his lodgings in Falkner Street, she suggested they should marry. And how my father had said he didn't know whether they should because there were 'certain things in his nature'.

She said she understood at once what he meant because there were many people in the theatre like that, including the Romeo in her production at Stratford, with whom she'd been very much in love. She told my father that it didn't matter. At that, she said, he seemed greatly relieved and they bought a bottle of wine and decided they were engaged. 'Of course,' she told us, 'I thought I could change him.' She said that without regret or remorse, more because it reminded her of how much she loved him than of how mistaken she was.

These are the familiar landmarks. But the unfamiliar waits just around the corner, ready to pounce, only wanting to hear a little intake of breath or an unguarded expression of surprise to know that one has been successfully ambushed. Like this inscription in the flyleaf of a book which I took down from my bookshelf only two days ago:

> . . . the word is love
> Surely one fearless kiss would cure
> The million fevers . . .
>
> For Mike
>   From Tommie
> Liverpool
> Jan 1940

The handwriting is not well formed, almost childish. He must have written his name 'Tommie' as a boy and still liked to spell it that way. But no child would have written an inscription like that, and no child would have chosen the *Selected Poems* of W. H. Auden as a gift.

The lines he quoted are from a stanza in a poem dedicated to Christopher Isherwood, 'Look, Stranger':

> Five summers pass and now we watch
> The Baltic from a balcony: the word is love.
> Surely one fearless kiss would cure
> The million fevers, a stroking brush
> The insensitive refuse from the burning core.
> Was there a dragon who had closed the works

While the starved city fed it with the Jews?
Then love would tame it with his trainer's look.

A pocket edition from the Faber Library, published in 1938, the price 3/6d pencilled in the inside cover. Was it bought in Liverpool to mark some occasion, or as a keepsake to remember him by? What was my father doing in Liverpool in January 1940? There is a reference in his diary to 'T's weekly visits' while *The Beggar's Opera* is on tour. It opened in London at the Haymarket Theatre in March 1940.

There is no entry for January in his diary. The last was for July 1939, the day that I was born, and there is no entry after that until 27 April 1940. It was a Saturday, and he was writing his diary in his dressing-room.

It was a hot day, and the prospect of two performances weighed him down. His make-up was elaborate; I know because Feliks Topolski did a series of cartoons showing every stage of his make-up for Macheath. Two fine pieces of gauze threaded with elastic were glued to the corner of his eyes with the strong Chinese lacquer such as dancers use. When the lacquer dried he took the two lengths of elastic threaded through the gauze and tied them as tightly as he could bear at the back of his head. They pulled the corners of his eyes up and outward. His appearance was almost oriental, or Slavic, giving the highwayman Macheath the look of a foundling of unknown parentage. Then came the wig. And that, for the time being, was that. He sat then for a while in his dressing-gown, asking those questions of his face in the mirror which helped to prepare him for the ordeal. Later he would put on the costume – as late as possible because it is heavy and stiff. The coat for the start of Act 2, for instance, is made of heavy blue felt.

I can see him very clearly writing his diary in that dressing-room at the Haymarket Theatre, because it has never changed. It is still the most beautiful dressing-room of any theatre in London, and I would love to use it myself. He writes:

Tomorrow down to Dedham to see T. He is staying there at the Cedric Morris School and working as a model. I am excited at the thought of the place, and the people, and of seeing him. A week ago, when it was suggested, I was afraid at the thought of all those young people. Am no longer. Also jealous of one of them. Must not be.

T is for Tommy then? Almost certainly.

The weekend goes extravagantly well. They are attending a painting school in the countryside which Constable made famous. Some are there as painters – Lucian Freud, David Carr; some are learning to paint; some are there as models – T and Millie Gummersall; some are there as visitors, in love with the models – my father and Stephen Spender (though Spender paints too). The whole atmosphere is so remote from war and fighting that at any moment you half expect an air raid in the distance to remind them that war had been declared eight months ago. But there is nothing of the kind; only the presence of a soldier, improbably called Boo, reminds you that this is April 1940.

In the afternoon T and I walked to Cedric Morris's house, about 2½ miles. A soldier (a late painter) called Boo. Sleepy and silent and smiling. Lovely house and garden. Millie and Stephen Spender (who had come over from Lavenham) and Lucian walked over just behind us. David came by car bringing Stephen's bike. Wild and amusing conversation.

By the time he leaves on the Monday, my father seems fathoms deep in love. I can hear the lilt in his voice, which comes at those rare moments when he is supremely happy, I can see his eyes glisten, and I know that he feels these moments so intensely because he knows they will not last.

T and I walked along the river in the morning past Angela Kinross, Lucian and David who were all painting at spots close to the Mill. It was an idyllic sort of walk. I can't even now remember what we said. T talked about *Esther Waters* at one moment, describing the end as happening in a meadow exactly like the one we were going through. I was blissfully happy and cannot and shall not try to describe the happiness beyond noting that at one moment I said to myself: tomorrow you will be in London, but if you are wise you can still be happy to think of this walk, and not sad and greedy.

Oddly I can get no sense of what Tommy is like, only that Michael loves him. Like that happiness which he does not want to describe, because to describe it might diminish it – it is something which can only be defined by its absence – so with Tommy. He will come into focus later, but at this moment there is such a golden glow surrounding him it is almost blinding.

The knowledge that I shall certainly see T again this week makes all the difference of course. When he went away, I was lost, and wild, and couldn't bring myself to work, or come home in good time.

On the left-hand pages of my father's diary are comments, and quotations from books he was reading at the time. In April 1940 he was reading André Gide's *Journal*, and there is one quotation from it which is peculiarly apt, though whether it was suggested by T specifically or whether Michael intends it for himself I am not sure. It is apt, however, in that it perfectly counter-points the reckless hedonism of that weekend, and no doubt many such weekends in time of war.

He wasn't insensitive. He was ignorant, immensely ignorant. He lacked sufficient imagination to be able to picture to himself what was happening in the basement or the kitchen while he was sitting in the dining-room. He is tender-hearted, I know, and cannot bear to see injustice. The trouble is he doesn't see very far. To carry on being happy and comfortable one must in fact not know how many thousands are suffering in order to preserve one's happiness.

As I read on in the diary I realise that he is referring this passage from Gide to himself. The problem with happiness, he discovers, is that one person's happiness is another's unhappiness. He tries to communicate what he is feeling to my mother.

On way to Piccadilly R asked me about Stephen S, his wife, Tommy's wife, etc. I always reply to her questions as fully as I can. She understands so much, but there is so much for her to understand.

The problem is not that she cannot understand. It is not even that my father is in love with a man. I think my mother would have been even more unhappy had he been in love with another woman. It is quite simply the fact that he is in love with two people. They are very different, different in temperament, outlook, upbringing, and he loves them in different ways. And he thinks he is needed by them both. And he cannot be in two places at once.

Saturday 4 May 1940.
Very tired and cross when we woke up, partly because R cried when we woke and we had sat till 3 or so talking things out. For two nights I have not been home and though I imagined that R knew where I was and accepted it it appears that I have caused her two days of agony. She talked at great length. She had been to see Edith [Evans]. I felt in despair with myself at my cruelty. Told R all about Roy and his end. Tried to explain the feeling of guilt I have towards her. Always it returns to this question of the split personality, and I cannot feel that it would be right – even if I had the will-power, which I have not – to cut off or starve the one side of my nature. I complained, weakly, but with some sense, that whereas people go to see plays like *Mourning Becomes Electra* and *The Family Reunion*, yet they think a person morbid who feels as those characters feel, and as I felt last night and have felt obscurely before: that I am the conscience of my unhappy family. Its bird sent flying through the purgatorial flame.

By midsummer it is over, for Michael at least; whether for Tommy I cannot tell.

Yesterday T came to lunch. Have seen very little of him lately. The great, deep feeling of love I had is no longer there. I feel only friendly, and have really lost a great deal of respect for him, which is, as much as anything else, the cause. He is a lonely, muddled creature, wanting always to turn back the clock. He spoke yesterday of wishing he had never left Wales, which meant that he would now be in the army and not have to think for himself. The real trouble also is that he cannot bring himself to work. The army (three years in the Guards) is largely responsible for this. He talked, after a while, freely about himself, and said there were only two people he could talk so to, me and S, but that S had forbidden him to talk of themselves for some time.

Bob Michell had been a conscripted soldier in the war, and had risen to the rank of sergeant. He had fought in the Pacific. He showed me a snapshot of himself in his GI uniform.

'Did you kill anyone in the war?' I asked.

'I never talk about that,' he said.

I had seen American soldiers during the war when we were evacuated in Bromyard. There must have been a transit camp nearby because a column of GIs often used to march down our road. There was a pretty girl who lived three doors away from us and once when she was standing on the pavement two of the soldiers pretended to have a fight over her.

Later there were American war movies. They were utterly different from the British ones, where the officers were decent and the men did their duty. In American films the soldiers, when they weren't actually fighting, thought and talked of nothing but girls – and they smoked all the time. The sergeants were extremely tough and wore very short crew-cuts.

There were exceptions to the toughness and ribaldry, but they were few and far between. Montgomery Clift was a shining exception. I had seen him in *The Search*, made just after the war. Later I saw him in *From Here to Eternity* and his performance made me cry. He played the soldier Robert Lee Pruitt who had been a champion boxer but had blinded his best friend in a bout of sparring and refused to box ever again.

I must have seen *From Here to Eternity* three times in the same week in 1953 at the Metropole, Victoria, and each time, when Montgomery Clift played the last post on the bugle, I was in tears. At the end the entire audience came out of the cinema weeping. The men didn't use handkerchiefs, but they didn't bother to disguise the fact that they were crying. As for the women, I have never seen so many handkerchiefs, and never heard so much sobbing in a film before or since.

Bob Michell was an exception too. He reminded me of Clift, because like him he was slow of speech and quite diffident, and though he looked strong and was strong he would never hit anyone, even in self-defence, unless he was terribly provoked. He didn't tell dirty stories and never wolf-whistled. So far as I knew he kept no pin-ups on the inside drawer of his wardrobe either. On the other hand I knew that women must think him immensely attractive. He had a dazzling smile, with the whitest teeth I had ever seen, even though he smoked a lot. He was lean and tall, about 6 feet 2 inches, almost as tall as my father. He had very dark, almost black hair, and high cheekbones. That was because he was an American Indian, he said – an Iroquois, and extremely proud of it.

I knew that women found him attractive because Vanessa told me so. It was the summer holidays in 1948 and we were back in Bromyard, staying at our cousin Lucy's. An older boy called Jimmy Nott and she used to dive into the bracken. Whenever I approached, they were always telling me to go and play somewhere else. Eventually I tackled Vanessa on the subject point-blank and asked her if she was in love with Jimmy Nott.

'Good heavens, no,' she said. 'Not with *him*.'

'Why not with him?' I asked.

'Because I'm in love with Bob Michell.'

I thought this was ridiculous and said so. Vanessa was eleven, and Bob was twice or three times her age.

'I know,' she said, in a faraway tone of voice which maddened me, as it was meant to. 'I think you'll find most women are in love with Bob.'

He came into our life in the summer of 1947, the hottest summer of the century. We were staying at the Wilton Court Hotel in Bexhill. That was the year my parents were in

Hollywood. Michael made two films, *The Secret Beyond the Door* directed by Fritz Lang, the other a film of Eugene O'Neill's *Mourning Becomes Electra*, for which he was nominated for an Oscar. Rachel made a film too, with Charles Boyer, *A Woman's Vengeance*, which was a version of Aldous Huxley's play *The Gioconda Smile*. We had begun our holiday without them. In August we had a wire to say that my father was coming back, on the *Queen Mary*, but that Rachel would return later as her film was delayed.

Every day at the seaside then was like the day before, except that the tide was an hour later. And except for the day my father arrived.

He was the proud possessor of a vintage 1936 Rolls-Royce, and his arrival at the Wilton Court Hotel on Marine Parade caused a tremendous stir. Nothing but whalemeat and suet pudding had been served all summer, but my father's sudden arrival on 9 August changed all that. Champagne appeared, potted shrimps were served, and all manner of forgotten delicacies danced their way out of the kitchen cupboards; and our waiter, who could balance two full plates on either arm and carry a third in either hand, was dancing and singing with them. Everyone was pleased to see my father, and we, who had not seen him for almost a year, were overjoyed. He brought pistols for all of us. Mine was a six-shooter, and the girls had antique-looking pirates' pistols, double-barrelled, with flint locks. He brought records of Ethel Merman in *Annie Get Your Gun*, and bubble gum and Milky Way. And he brought a friend with him, Bob Michell.

Bob played with us every day. He always played with a cigarette in his mouth, holding it between his teeth. He even swam on his back with a cigarette between his teeth. He was completely unlike all my father's other friends, and as far as I was concerned he beat them all into a cocked hat. Others like Dick Green, my father's friend from Cambridge days, often came and stayed. Dick was charming, but quite hopeless. He also smoked incessantly, even on the beach, but he'd never

learned to master it as Bob did. The smoke would curl up into
Dick's eyes so that he always squinted sideways at you, and
when ash formed on the end of his cigarette he never seemed
to notice until it was too late and the ash had fallen on his
chest or on to the carpet. He had a terrible cough, and was no
good at getting up in the morning because he had always drunk
too much the night before. He always used long words and
treated me as if he thought I was very intelligent, which flattered
me, so that I didn't dare to ask him what he meant in case he
realised I was not. One conversation I remember with Dick
from that time, and it was completely incomprehensible to me.

'Are you a believer?' he asked me.

'I think I am,' I answered cautiously. 'Are you?'

'Oh no,' said Dick, screwing up his eyes, and laughing like
a drain until he coughed. 'Not at all. I always say, what's wrong
with good old humanism?'

Dick was nice, but absolutely useless at playing games, swimming or anything at all except lying on the beach and smoking.
Whereas Bob, from that first evening, wanted to play with us
and never grew tired of it. Even Lynn, who was shy with adults,
and didn't walk much because our nanny thought she suffered
from anaemia and kept her in a pushchair, soon lost her shyness
with Bob. Cigarette between his teeth, he ran with her pushchair the whole length of Marine Parade, up to the De La Warr
Pavilion and back.

He also saved me from drowning. There were two drowning
episodes that summer, Vanessa's and mine – only Vanessa's
was heroic, whereas mine was shameful. She, who was a strong
swimmer, saw a much older girl in difficulties some way out
to sea, swam out and rescued her. The girl's parents made a
tremendous fuss of Vanessa, and the *Brighton and Hove Argus*
carried a front-page story and a picture of her with the girl she
rescued. As for me, I found myself drowning only a few inches
out of my depth. I hadn't long learned to swim, and shouldn't
have been out of my depth, but there I was. I grew tired of
swimming back to the shore and the water kept closing over my

head. I felt embarrassed at having to call for help but reckoned I must, and with each mouthful of air I shouted, yet no one came until two arms lifted me out of the water and laid me down on the shore. It was Bob, smiling so that his eyes crinkled up and almost disappeared.

'You were trying to frighten me,' he said.

I begged him not to tell anyone, and he didn't.

In the evenings, after Lynn had gone to bed, Bob, my father, Vanessa and I played gin rummy. And after we had gone to bed they would head off to play darts and shove-halfpenny in The Bell.

At the end of that summer Bob disappeared, and we forgot about him until the next year, when it turned out he was living in the studio round the corner from our house. The house was huge, but not big enough for my father, who always needed somewhere to get away to – somewhere he could read and write, and especially somewhere he could rest without being disturbed.

First he restored an old ruined gazebo at the bottom of the garden, and he worked there for a while. He was writing in his spare time, all through the autumn of 1947 and the following year, a play called 'Juliana' and he was very modest about it. Later he restored the original title of the story he had adapted from Henry James, *The Aspern Papers*.

Even in the gazebo he was still liable to be invaded by noise from the garden, so he moved his work to a beautiful studio he bought in Church Street, just round the corner from Chiswick Mall. That was where Bob came to live on his second visit. I fell upon him and demanded to know why he had been away so long, almost a year. He couldn't explain, or said it was too complicated, having to do with permits and passports. Life had been quite dull without him, and I told him he ought to stay longer this time. He said he would if he could.

Bob had worked for Western Union, the American cable company, on the west coast, but his ambition was to be an actor. The US government had given him a GI grant for training, and he was able to spend that abroad, so he had enrolled as a mature drama student at the Central School, which at that time was high up in the dome of the Albert Hall in Kensington.

He studied for a year, but after that he had only one part as a professional actor, and the play opened and closed while I was at boarding-school so I never saw him. But he still lived in our studio for the next eight years, until 1956. He used to drive my father, who never drove except on his honeymoon. Gradually he lost almost all his American accent, and I noticed that he looked more and more like my father. He went to the same tailor, though not as often as Michael, who was extravagant with clothes. He even took to smoking a pipe, again like my father, though he never looked comfortable with it.

Gradually, though his eyes still smiled, I noticed that the rest of his face looked sad. Being an Iroquois Indian he had skin that was very smooth, and he never had a grey hair on his head, but I noticed deep furrows on his forehead. One evening he fainted and couldn't be revived until an ambulance came, and they pumped his chest and rubbed his hands.

When the time came for him to leave he cried for days, quite noiselessly and always smiling a little. The day before he left he held my face in his hands and said, 'I will never forget you children.' I was sixteen then, and said, with all seriousness, that I would never forget him. And I never did, though to my burning shame I realised after I had learned of his death that I had never answered his letters, and though I had once written him a very long letter, a short book almost, when I was eighteen, all about my problems, I never posted it because when I reread it I didn't like it, or didn't think it did me justice.

I don't know why Bob left – perhaps because he wanted to have children of his own. He went back to his job in the Western Union, married and had two children. My mother met him in America at some point and said he was very happy because he had always wanted to be a father. My father met him too, much later, in Reno in the 1970s. Michael was on a tour of the States, and Bob must have contacted him and told him he was ill. My father had Parkinson's disease by then, and his appearance must have been a shock to Bob. So too must Bob's have been. The cigarette he always stuck between his teeth was killing him. The doctors had removed his larynx and he had to communicate with a little notepad.

I never thought anyone would replace Bob in our family, but I was wrong. My father returned from America in the summer of 1956, after a successful season on Broadway as Hector in Jean Giraudoux's *Tiger at the Gates*. He had made friends with a young actor and director called Fred Sadoff. Soon after Michael's return Fred came to London to direct a play at the Arts Theatre. For a short while he too lived in the studio in Church Street. But this was the year when my father had to sell both house and studio in Chiswick to settle old tax demands, so when we moved Fred had to move also.

We moved to a huge ugly flat in Hans Crescent overlooking Harrods, and Fred found a small flat nearby in Egerton Gardens Mews. His production at the Arts Theatre had been modestly successful, but he had difficulty getting a permit to work as an actor, and was still too unknown and untried to find work as a director.

At seventeen I was still as much in love with America and Americana as I had been at eight, and the simple fact that Fred was American was for me a great point in his favour. As a young star of Lee Strasberg's Actors' Studio he knew and could tell stories of Marlon Brando, Eva Marie Saint, Ben Gazzara and Antony Franciosa. He could talk knowledgeably about the 'Method', or Strasberg's version of it. All this made him fascinating company, and for two years I saw him almost every day. He used to confide in me when my father was particularly distant and uncommunicative, and gradually it dawned upon me what their relationship was. 'Gradually' is a much over-used word, but I cannot avoid it here because, as in John Donne's description of a friend's death, there was no moment, no single discovery of which I could say: that was it, that was the instant in which I realised that my father was gay.

There were discoveries of a sort, but however obvious they seem as I write them now I drew no conclusions from them. I simply noted them. I read, without meaning to, a letter from Rachel to my father, in which she referred to Fred as 'your lover'. I saw the way my father managed to include Fred in some capacity in almost every job he did — sometimes with peculiar consequences. He accompanied my parents with the Shakespeare Memorial Company to Moscow in 1958, and one night in the Metropole Hotel he was arrested and taken away for questioning by the KGB. Fred, whose only political action had been to vote for Adlai Stevenson against Eisenhower, was astonished, terrified and utterly bewildered when his interrogator pointed out that his name was Sadoff, the same as Lev Davidovich Trotsky's son, Leon Sedov.

When my father became ill, at the beginning of the 1970s, Fred returned to America. He must have had great difficulty making a living there. He was no longer young, and had no successes to his name of the kind which would open doors for him in Hollywood or New York.

Some people thought he used my father, and in a way he did. But I think all the same he got no more from their relationship than he gave. Though he could never replace Bob in my father's life, he gave a great deal. Indomitably cheerful, funny, loyal after a fashion, he died of AIDS last year.

IO

Explanations

❦

It was midnight and Michael and I were talking in the drawing-room of my parents' flat in Hans Crescent. Earlier that evening we had gone to the Fortune Theatre to see Arbuzov's *The Promise*; Michael and I, Fred Sadoff and Lehman Engel. The others had gone home, and Michael was telling me about Lehman and his troubles – a brilliant musician who was all too often, my father said, unhappily in love. 'Lehman, as you've probably guessed, is homosexual.' I made no answer to this information. It was more or less superfluous. Lehman was indeed obviously, openly, triumphantly homosexual. My father sighed, the clock above the mantelpiece struck twelve, and he fell silent.

I was intending to stay the night with my parents. It was 1967, and my second child, Luke, had been born two nights before, on 9 April. My first wife Deirdre and he were tucked up for the night in Queen Charlotte's maternity hospital in Hammersmith. My daughter Jemma was staying with Deirdre's parents, who had come over from Malta for the birth of their second grandchild. Our flat felt lonely without them and I thought to spend the next few nights with my parents, in the bedroom I had left five years before. Perhaps I wanted to recapture a taste of my childhood, or at least my adolescence, in the narrow bed which had been mine, on and off, until the day I married in July 1962.

It was an eventful time. Both my sisters had been nominated

for Oscars at the beginning of the year, Vanessa for *Morgan –
A Suitable Case for Treatment*, Lynn for *Georgy Girl*. A sudden
flurry of journalists descended upon my father, wanting to
interview him as the father of the clan. He enjoyed the attention. But he remained, despite all the attention and publicity,
watchful and critical. About Vanessa's performances and mine
he was, however proud or impressed, invariably astringent:
'Wrote a longish letter to Vanessa congratulating her on her TV
programme and suggesting her smoking is ruining her voice';
'Rachel and I in the evening to *A Man for All Seasons*. Corin
very good. Strong. His eyes are a little close together I notice
for the first time.' Only Lynn, like Matthew Arnold's Shakespeare, no longer abides his question; and for her he can feel
uninhibitedly proud and loving: 'At Wells, to see Lynn's film
Georgy Girl which makes me weep with laughter and affection.
I love that girl.'

Lynn was married in New York at the beginning of April
1967, in Sidney Lumet's flat, by a minister from the Ethical
Church, and Michael had flown over for 'the occasion' to 'give
her away' to her husband John Clark. It touched me, even then,
how conventionally excited he became, or rather how he liked
to convey his pleasure and excitement in these conventional
patriarchal expressions. And now another moment of patriarchal pride: the birth of his fourth grandchild.

He himself, if not quite at the peak of his career, was not
far from it. All sorts of unexpectedly challenging work was
proposed to him that year: Lord Cardigan in Tony Richard-
son's film of *The Charge of the Light Brigade*; Federico Fellini's
new film, in which to play a dead cellist who thinks he is still
alive (the story was filmed, in fact, much later, and became
The Orchestra); a new Broadway musical with a score by the
great Jule Styne. But he turned them all down, hardly giving
them a second glance. He seemed to prefer a week's highly
paid work in a run-of-the-mill adventure film, or a commentary
for a television documentary. He wanted to lie fallow, spending
weeks at a time at his friend Dick Green's house in Somerset,

drinking Black Velvet, or Screwdrivers, or Planter's Punch, playing cards and talking until all hours with the circle of old friends who kept their orbit around Dick.

Physically he looked astonishingly well kept. At fifty-nine he had no grey in his hair. What thickness there was about his waist he kept in check by daily walking and running, two or three miles, in Somerset or along the Serpentine. There were hints of the illness to come, but nothing more, and he could still dismiss them as minor inconveniences. At least he pretended he could. His memory was unreliable and he found he needed to take notes of anything if he wanted to remember it for more than five minutes. And he had recurring bouts of giddiness. Earlier in the year he had been to the Fortune Theatre, to see the same play, *The Promise*, but had had to leave before the third act because he had collapsed in the second interval, crashing to the floor as he was leaving the foyer to take some air. His doctor said it was low blood pressure, and advised him to take more exercise and drink less.

I cannot remember how he introduced the subject when, after an interminably long pause during which each of us, it seemed, had become absorbed in his own thoughts, he spoke again. Probably there was no introduction. I remember that his breathing seemed strained and difficult.

'I think I ought to tell you', he said, 'that I am, to say the least of it, bisexual.'

I recall every syllable of that sentence, with its strange qualification 'to say the least of it', because it took him an age to say it and the pauses, which were more or less as I have punctuated them, were painful. In each pause he breathed more deeply, to the bottom of his lungs, letting the air out with a punctured sigh, his shoulders sagging forward. When he had finished he stared at me, angrily, as if I had forced him to speak, as if I had taken advantage of his too trusting nature, and then came three huge, heaving sobs, 'Aaagh ... aaagh ... aaagh', and then the dam burst and his grief and rage came out in a great, terrible, heaving cascade.

Explanations

I had often seen my father cry. He cried freely, without any attempt at restraint, and I was always grateful to have learned from him that there is nothing wrong with crying; quite the contrary. But I had never seen him cry like this. It was beyond anything I had experienced, a grief so awful that it seemed to undo him.

I sat on the arm of his armchair, folded my arms around his neck, and when eventually he quietened a little I said, 'I know.' He said, 'Do you?' And that was all. The end of the conversation.

When we spoke again it was as if the subject had never been mentioned or thought of. I sat on the edge of his armchair and saw his face change like a panorama of the seasons from watery sunshine to the summer sun in all its splendour. We had a brandy, talked about nothing in particular, and went to bed, he to his large bedroom at the bend of the corridor where the pillows were piled high, I to the small bedroom at the end of the corridor, where for a long time I lay and thought.

I had said, 'I know', but did I? Had he simply named something which I knew already but had never spoken? Or had he in naming it changed my understanding? I had some knowledge of a sort, gathered empirically and often accidentally, but what did it amount to, where had I kept it, what had I done with it, and why had I not named it until now? I knew, for instance, didn't I, that my father had lovers, men like Bob and now Fred? If I thought about it I could see that there must have been scores more, for a day, or a night, or longer. Some, maybe, with an intensity of affection that might have matched his love for Bob.

The more I lay awake thinking the more it seemed to me, comfortingly, that perhaps I had known this all my life. I remembered an evening at Chiswick, when I was thirteen or fourteen, and after dinner my father had read aloud to us from the diary he had kept at school. He made it sound very funny, sending himself up, and my mother was laughing till the tears ran down and begged him to read on. His reading became a comic *tour de force*. Now and then he would do a double-take at whatever it was that he had been about to read, and say in a singsong voice, 'Yes, well, perhaps we'll skip that part', and turn several pages at once. After a while, despite our pleas, he put the book down and read from something else.

Days later, prowling about the house when it was empty one afternoon I found his school diary and began to read it myself, looking of course for those parts which he had skipped. They were about his friends, his jealousies and rivalries. They did not seem exceptional. I could see nothing shameful about them. At Westminster where I was at school there were jokes that this one was in love with that one, was sending secret messages, or had proposed a 'dirty weekend'. All that was part of my daily experience and I could see no difference between that and what my father was writing about at Clifton, except that he wrote about it rather solemnly, in utter seriousness, whereas in my experience it was usually treated as a furtive joke.

One episode, however, was unlike the rest because my father was clearly ashamed of it. He was on holiday in Paris with Andy and his half-sister Peg. It was the summer of 1925, so he must have been seventeen. On this particular evening after the others had gone to bed he put on his hat and went out walking. He passed a man and noticed that he was looking at him. They started talking. The man was Italian, respectably but shabbily dressed, and they couldn't understand a word each other said. They walked back to his lodgings, in a little dark street somewhere behind the Rue de Clichy, and up the stairs to his room, not much bigger than a cupboard. His breath smelled strongly of garlic. In a moment Michael was overcome with shame and fear, seized his hat, threw some money in the man's face and ran downstairs to the street.

There I ran. Ran hard, with panting chest and burning shameful cheeks, muttering at every step, 'Fool! Fool! Fool!' I took hours to find my way back to the hotel. I cursed myself for a soddish idiot. I got into bed and slept, my heart beating with reproachful shame, my eyes shut tight to blot out the remembrance of my sordidness.

This, obviously, he had not wanted me to see. Or had he? Had he meant by reading his diary aloud, leaving out those bits whose contents I could only guess at, to lay a trail for me which might, as in fact it had, lead me at some moment in his absence to make this discovery?

And what had I discovered? What had he and the little Italian done or been about to do in that little room no bigger than a cupboard?

I wanted to know more, but it was difficult. My great friend at school, Michael Wolchover, was a year or so older than I and tremendously precocious. He had several girlfriends and was more than happy to tell me about his experiences with them in some detail. But he also said he had a relationship with a man, a jazz singer called Tommy, who he said had an enormous cock. I asked him what he did with it, but my friend was tiresomely reticent and said, 'I couldn't possibly tell you.'

I read very widely at this time, looking for instruction or at least enlightenment. One source was the Penguin edition of Plato's *Symposium*, with an introduction by my headmaster Walter Hamilton. It was all about love between men. It looked not unlike my father's world, I thought, peopled by a cast of beautiful young men and older men, and one old man who was infallibly wise and so repulsively ugly that he was almost sublimely attractive. I could have cast Plato's dialogue with ease from among my father's friends. The producer 'Binkie' Beaumont I cast as Alcibiades, Arthur Marshall or Paul Dehn as Aristophanes. Socrates was not so easy. The most likely candidate, though not entirely satisfactory, was Sir Dennis Robertson, who often came to stay. He was a bachelor with a bald head which poked in and out of his shoulders like a tortoise. He was a distinguished economist and was appointed at about this time by the government to head a brains trust of three advisers to the Treasury. The press instantly dubbed them 'the three wise men', so in that respect at least he was suitable casting.

'We have to face the fact,' wrote my headmaster, 'however

unpalatable it may be, that in Periclean Athens love between men was an accepted ideal.' Why should it be so unpalatable? At what point did love become unpalatable – or, worse, shameful, illegal, a punishable crime?

I read Montgomery Hyde's *Trials of Oscar Wilde*. It was gripping. I wanted to cheer at every clever retort Wilde made from the witness box.

'Never mind your doctor, sir.'

'I never do.'

I hated Wilde's 'prose poem' to Lord Alfred Douglas, which was one long purple passage. 'Your slim gilt soul walks between passion and poetry' sounded dressed up, effete, and reminded me of the illustrations in Arthur Rackham's *Green Fairy Book* which Vanessa loved and I loathed. But I thoroughly applauded Wilde's brave-spirited defence of 'the love that dares not speak its name'. Only why should it not dare, and what would its name be if it dared?

Its proper name I learned was homosexuality, usually pronounced 'hŏm-er-sexuality' with a short 'o' by the chaplain and others in authority to emphasise their manly distaste for the subject. I learned in fact to distinguish an unacknowledged conflict between two camps, the short 'o's and the long 'o's, as in hōmōsexual. In the camp of the short 'o's was my housemaster, twice married, with two children and a long red beard; the chaplain, also married; and Mr Hamerton, in charge of rowing, unmarried, and suspected of being a latent long 'o'. In the camp of the long 'o's was my classics master, Theodore Tzinn. He taught us Hadrian's epigram, 'Homo sum, et nihil humanum alienum puto', where to further complicate things 'hŏmō' was pronounced with a short 'o' and a long 'o', but no matter. He was a bachelor and much the best of my teachers. Consciously or not he was very Socratic in his method, walking round and round the courtyard with us, endlessly discussing, constantly questioning.

It also dawned upon me that homosexuality was a disease, an illness. This I learned from the trial of Lord Montagu and his friends, and more extensively from Peter Wildeblood, one of the defendants, in his book *Against the Law*. It is a plea for tolerance and understanding, and against the cruelty of imprisonment. However, on the central question which was the nature of the 'crime' he was imprisoned for, Wildeblood seemed to agree with his captors. It was an illness.

This indeed solved the problem. What logic could there be for locking up a person if what they had done was acknowledged to be the expression of an illness? Clearly, if that was what it was, imprisonment was barbaric.

But in solving one problem it revealed another, altogether more alarming problem. If homosexuality was an illness, how could you catch it? How could you learn to recognise the symptoms in yourself or others, and could you recognise them in time, and could you prevent them or, if that were too late, could you cure them? All these questions troubled me a lot, so much at times that I almost returned to religion, hoping that prayer might save me.

I do not know whether I applied this contradiction to Michael, but it seemed to me that evening in 1967 that I must have done, and that I had applied it to him gratefully, in order to absolve him. Because how could a man so obviously strong and healthy be suffering from disease? Like a simple syllogism it proved, at whatever unconscious level my adolescence had been demanding proof, that he was normal.

I I

What I Thought I Knew

☥

Alan Turing, the mathematician who cracked the Enigma code and the father of the modern computer, committed suicide by biting on a poisoned apple dipped in cyanide on 7 June 1954. He had been convicted two years before of gross indecency under section 11 of the Criminal Law Amendment Act (1885), the same statute which had been used to imprison Oscar Wilde and many thousands of gay men since. Turing himself was not sentenced to prison. He was bound over for a year on probation, on the condition that he agreed to submit to 'organotherapy', which meant injection with the female sex hormone oestrogen.

Some experiments in America, where castration was still prescribed in eleven states as both punishment and cure, had been made in the 1940s with forcible injection of the male hormone testosterone. But when it was found that this only had the effect of increasing the libido of the gay men without changing their sexual orientation, it was decided that the goal of treatment should be to eliminate sexual desire altogether. And it was proposed to do this by injecting gay men with oestrogen. The first British scientific paper on the subject appeared almost a decade later, in the *Lancet* in 1949. Its authors claimed that their experiments on thirteen men, using large doses of oestrogen, proved that 'libido could be abolished within a month'.

Turing had told the police who questioned him that he thought a 'government commission had been set up to recommend changes in the law'. He was wrong. Public attitudes may have been changing, becoming slowly more tolerant, but prosecutions were on the increase. Lord Montagu, who like Turing had reported a minor theft to the police, found himself in turn charged with indecency. His case became a public show trial in the autumn of 1953. The trial ended in December that year, without conviction, but Montagu was rearrested, with Peter Wildeblood, in January 1954, this time charged with an offence said to have been committed two years previously. All the trappings of these trials suggested that the state was determined to secure convictions. The Special Branch was involved; dangers to the morals of the armed forces were alleged; conscripts in the RAF gave evidence for the prosecution and claimed to have been seduced. Telephones were tapped. Prosecution witnesses were coerced, first with the stick of prosecution for themselves if they should be unhelpful, then with the carrot of immunity if they co-operated. The Home Secretary, Sir David Maxwell Fyfe, briefed magistrates on the government's insistence that there be a 'drive against male vice'.

Although Turing was wrong in thinking that a government-appointed committee was considering changes in the law, such a committee was appointed after his death, in the autumn of 1954, and it may be that his suicide was a contributing factor. Sir John Wolfenden, the Vice-Chancellor of Reading University, was invited by Maxwell Fyfe to head the committee. In his autobiography, *Turning Points*, Wolfenden describes his first meeting with Maxwell Fyfe, in a first-class sleeper on the night train to London from Liverpool. Fyfe, who was in his dressing-gown and little else, told Wolfenden that one of the reasons for examining the law against male homosexuality was that 'two cases had attracted considerable public notice'. The cases are not specified. Neither Turing's conviction nor his suicide had attracted much press and public attention, so it seems unlikely that they were implied. Yet both must have shaken the academic and scientific community, especially those who were connected with atomic research and with the security services.

Nor does Wolfenden make clear whether Maxwell Fyfe – whose record as Home Secretary is especially harsh, including his refusal of pleas for clemency for Derek Bentley – was envisaging that the proposed committee would in due course recommend changes in the direction of more liberalisation, or whether it would advocate heavier punishments. Probably the latter. 'Nobody had any idea how much of it there was, because it was, for obvious reasons, normally conducted in private. But there was an impression that it was increasing; and there was a feeling that it ought to be curbed.' Such is Wolfenden's précis of Maxwell Fyfe's preamble.

The outlook of a man who can say or write, without conscious irony, that gay activity is 'normally' conducted in private 'for obvious reasons' can hardly be guessed at. What obvious reasons could there be, apart from the traditional one that public buggery frightens the horses? Nevertheless Wolfenden formed his committee, which of course did not include any known gay person, though it took a great deal of oral evidence and read a great deal more, 'and pretty sickening reading it was'.

Wolfenden's report was published in 1957, and after Beveridge's it must head the list of all-time bestsellers published by Her Majesty's Stationery Office. There are other similarities. True, Wolfenden never became a public hero like Beveridge – rather the contrary. In his dry, unemphatic way he had to endure sheaves of anonymous poison-pen letters, graffiti daubed on the walls of his house in Reading and thunderous attacks from the press. Certainly he can't be said to have changed as many lives for the better as Beveridge. But he brought comfort to millions of men, including my father. Almost as clearly as I remember the day ten years later when he told me that he was bisexual, I remember my father reading the evening newspaper on the day Wolfenden's report was published.

There was almost a decade between these two days, 2 September 1957 and 11 April 1967. Introducing the bill which became the Sexual Offences Act of 1967, Leo Abse made the point that under the law as it stood homosexuals comprised, next to motorists, the largest class of criminals in the land. This overwhelming disparity between the actual number of crimes presumably committed each day and the minute percentage against which the police were able to enforce the law, as well as the invasion of privacy which would be needed if they seriously tried to enforce the law in all cases, was the first reason Abse gave for changing the law. Only after that came the need for compassion in cases involving consenting adults over the age of twenty-one, for those 'who suffer the appalling misfortune of being a homosexual': 'For most of them there can be no question that they are permanently denied the blessings of family life, the gifts and rewards of parenthood, the gift of a mature love with a woman.'

My father, who was not denied any of these blessings – I think he really believed they were blessings, though he would not have used the high moral tone which Abse resorted to – was nevertheless vulnerable to Abse's third reason, which was blackmail. He was especially vulnerable perhaps as a married man with children.

As I recall that evening in 1967, it seems to me therefore, despite all appearances to the contrary, a happy occasion. I know that hindsight often bestows a fullness of vision quite at odds with one's perception of an event at the moment it happened. Perhaps, at the time, I was shocked – not by what my father told me, but at how painful it was for him to tell it.

Did he feel that he was in danger of exposure and want to warn me in advance before the blow fell? Unlikely. In fact at no time before or since could he have been less in danger. His loves and his adventures were all in private between consenting adults and would very soon become lawful; and the risk of blackmail was minimal now that his family were grown up.

Rather, it must have been because the danger which had

threatened him all his young life was now receding and would soon become, at least for a short while, a memory that he felt compelled to speak, to say what he had never been able to say before. I hope he was not afraid that I would be shocked. And I hope especially that if he was afraid he was comforted to find that I wasn't shocked. I cling to these hopes like rafts, because of course there is no way of confirming them. It would be truly awful to imagine any other scenario.

I believe that my father wanted me to know what he had never been able to bring himself to say before and would never talk about again, and that the pain and grief of that moment was the accumulated pain of all the things he'd felt himself unable to say before. Society had forced him to live, for more than thirty years, a life of concealment. Family life for him was not a disguise, not some artificial construct to divert attention from his real self. It was as true and as real as his love for Bob, or Fred. But the prejudice and repression of his time had forced him to live two lives, against his nature.

Years later I made a great mistake and gave an interview to a journalist from the *Independent on Sunday*. The mistake was not that I chose the wrong newspaper, but that I decided to overlook what was almost a settled conviction that no interview had ever brought me anything but discomfort and I had best avoid them entirely. I yielded on this occasion because the play I was about to appear in, Ibsen's *Rosmersholm*, had never been popular and I was persuaded that publicity would help it. And perhaps, if I am to be scrupulously truthful, I was curious to see whether, after such a long abstinence – this was 1992 and I had not given an interview for fifteen years – the face which would emerge would be more recognisably mine, at least to me. Vanity, I know, comes in all shapes and sizes, and the vainest man is one who never looks at himself in the mirror, wanting to preserve eternally his inner image of himself. Perhaps he deserves everything he gets.

The young woman who interviewed me was so much better dressed and better looking than I that I wondered whether our roles had not been accidentally reversed. Her questions made me feel more and more uncomfortable, as if I were being asked to pick my nose in the middle of Piccadilly Circus – questions such as 'Do you like yourself?' or 'Do you think you are a good actor?' But I tried to hide my dismay, to deflect where I could, to answer what I had to, and generally to treat her questions with a respect I hardly thought they deserved. Often they seemed to me to be based on what other journalists had said about me, and when I tried to steer away from these she said, 'One has to start somewhere.'

The face which emerged when the interview was published was that of a humourless chronic depressive, and I was bound to think that if that was the face I showed then my decision not to do interviews was plain common sense, and breaking my rule was the utmost folly, more likely to drive audiences away from Ibsen than attract them.

Yet in one respect it was especially galling. The journalist had interviewed, as part of the 'background' to my interview, my first wife, and had got from her a very different account of that conversation with my father in 1967:

> She recalls a night, before Corin joined the party, when he was telephoned by his father, who wanted to see him privately and alone. When Corin returned late that night he said to her: 'I am going to tell you something now and it shall never be mentioned again.' His father had just informed him that he had homosexual relationships all his life. 'You can imagine, can't you, that he felt a fool, felt betrayed,' she says . . . Perhaps all you can say is that it is never possible to grasp another's grief. It must have occurred to Corin that his politics is some vast superstructure designed to conceal his desperation.

It was embarrassing to read in an otherwise intelligent newspaper an 'explanation' of revolutionary politics such as this; but far more galling to see, in black and white, this version of my father's homosexual relationships according to which I felt a fool, felt betrayed.

I wrote a private letter of protest which was answered, but so blandly and unapologetically that I felt even worse about the business. I told myself that not many people would have read the interview, and very few indeed would remember it for more than an hour or two – all of which was true. But some damage had been done, and I, in a way, had contributed by agreeing to the interview. What had been said could not be unsaid, except by the most laborious process of denial. And however few had read it I felt it might have contributed, for those who read it uncritically, to the growing menace of an attempt, which was then taking shape, to undo the very limited rights which had been won for gay people. This climate of opinion would prejudice the right, which has never been securely established, for gay people to have and raise children, their own or by adoption. It would make bisexual men and women hypocrites and deceivers, instead of what they are, which is people who do those things which for others are only done in fantasy and imagination.

It is quixotic to tilt at windmills, and especially quixotic to revisit old battlefields, where the grass has grown over the graves, and the cries of the injured and the dying have faded into the wind. But I must assert that I found my father, on that night of his confession, and that what I found was a real, not a 'pretended family relationship' as the Local Government Act would have it. And though I often lost it subsequently in the way one does, from time to time, I could always find it again.

12

Acting Hamlet

❦

It was the summer of 1958, the third season my father spent at Stratford, and he was playing Hamlet and Benedick. My mother played Lady Capulet, Ursula in *Much Ado About Nothing* and Dionysa in *Pericles*.

Stratford was teeming with tourists and souvenir shops to take their money, but it was a cottage industry compared to today's. There was no Hilton Hotel to the right of the Clopton bridge. The shops, most of them, were the kind of drapers and ironmongers and utility stores which could be found in any market town of comparable size. Their customers were mainly local inhabitants.

There was only one theatre, the Shakespeare Memorial Theatre. It had been built in the early 1930s after the old Victorian structure had burned to the ground. It was referred to irreverently as the 'jam factory', and in its unromantic way it did look quite like the kind of new-model factories which used to line the Great West Road in the 1930s and 1940s.

For years a certain smell would greet you the moment you entered its foyer. It was so rare and so distinctive, like the smell of the Paris Metro, that if one were to awake in such a place, blindfold and disorientated, one sniff would give the place away. It greeted you as you entered the foyer and stayed with you as you turned left, past the fountain at the well of the stairway, and up the winding stairs to the dress circle or the restaurant. I don't know whether it belonged to the polish which was used on the stone-flagged floors or whether its source was buried deep in the Bedfordshire bricks of the building itself. When I visited the theatre last, a year ago, I fancied it was still there but I could not be sure because too many counter-smells were wafted from the well-dressed audience. One would have needed to visit the place in the morning or at dead of night to be certain. To be sentimental, I would call it the smell of Shakespeare.

Or, rather, one of the smells of Shakespeare. The other, no less distinctive, had nothing in common with stone-flagged floors and Shakespeare's coat of arms. It was the smell of Shakespeare the actor. It was compounded of the size used to prime the canvas and the wood of the sets, the felt and leather which were used for the costumes, hung row upon row in racks under dust-sheets, sweat and greasepaint. I feel almost embarrassed to name this last commodity in a world which had grown cynical about actors without ever having learned to love them, and 'greasepaint' undeniably sounds camp. But greasepaint did smell, especially Leichner's, which was still very much in use then, and it was part of the equally unforgettable odour which haunted the stage-door of the Shakespeare Memorial Theatre and spread itself through the whole of the theatre backstage, into the green-room and up into the dressing-rooms.

It was the last of three seasons my parents acted at Stratford and 1958 was the last year of my boyhood. I had left school the previous December and was going to Cambridge in the autumn. I spent the first of those free nine months at Stratford – when the crocuses and daffodils were coming out and the actors were still rehearsing – and most of the summer too. I did all the things I had always done at Stratford, rowing and punting on the river so much that I knew every bend and contour of the Avon between Stratford and Alveston, but I did them differently and distractedly because I was in love.

A film called *High Society* with songs by Cole Porter had appeared not long before, and in one scene Bing Crosby was tying his tie in a mirror, singing about the woman he loved,

Grace Kelly. The song was called 'I love you, Samantha', and it was bitter-sweet because Crosby's character wasn't sure at that point in the story whether Samantha/Grace Kelly loved him. That seemed to fit my situation exactly. I walked for hours round the rainy lanes between Alveston and Tiddington, warbling Crosby's song and thinking about Dorothy Tutin. The film had a happy ending. My story, I knew perfectly well, wouldn't. I had been in love with Tutin ever since I had seen her play Joan in Jean Anouilh's *The Lark*, and I besieged her all winter with presents, letters, invitations and phone calls, but with no success, except sometimes to hold her hand. She was playing Juliet, and the actor playing Romeo was older than I, more handsome, more assured and, as I bitterly, jealously, secretly knew, much more likely to be successful in his pursuit of her than I.

Hamlet, in which she played Ophelia, opened while I was abroad. Michael was fifty, an age when most leading actors would have been content to put away the rapier and dagger and settle into the role of Claudius or even Polonius. But Glen Byam Shaw, the theatre's director, had persuaded him to have one more try – his third – at the part.

I was in France when the play opened, and probably for the first time in my young life I was far enough away, and sufficiently distracted by my own pursuits and interests, not to feel nervous for him. His success had always mattered to me so much before that I would put myself through all kinds of rituals in the hope they would somehow bring success to him. As time went on these rituals became more and more complicated and esoteric. But I knew that I must observe them minutely, and that provided I did I could almost write the reviews which would appear the following morning. Success, when it came, in the shape of good reviews, was its own reward. Certainly it brought me some relief. But the corollary of so much anxiety for success was that when it didn't come I felt responsible for my father's failure.

He had written to me once or twice at Versailles, where I

was staying. Fifty is a time of life, I have since discovered, when one starts to joke about one's age, hoping that no one else will. I can detect something of this in what I remember of my father's letters to me. In one of them he says that he has just had a 'champagne rinse' before having Angus McBean take a photograph of him in costume, 'and I am pleased to say I don't look a day older than fifty'.

Fifty would not have seemed improbably elderly in my grandfather's day for an actor to play Hamlet. In those days if an actor conquered a part and made it his own, he expected it to stay with him for the rest of his life. Sir John Martin-Harvey had a lifetime's monopoly in the role of Sidney Carton, which he played 5,004 times, the last being in his seventy-sixth year. But by the time Michael played Hamlet at fifty rock and roll and much else had appeared and he was in danger of being beached by this first wave of youth culture – or so he felt. At any rate it was a moot point. Most of the critics didn't mention his age, but you sensed there was some degree of politeness in that. Kenneth Tynan, the best of the theatre critics then, and the first to look for and identify new trends, mentioned it, rather caustically. 'At fifty', he wrote, 'Redgrave is the oldest actor to assay the role since Aimee Blanchard struck a glancing blow for femininity by playing it at 59.' Tynan's notice was respectful, apart from this joke and one or two others, but not enthusiastic.

He suggested in one of his irritating *obiter dicta* that an actor's eyes were the most important part of his physical equipment, and that Redgrave's problem was that he was one-eyed, like the Cyclops. He praised his mind and his taste, but backhandedly, suggesting that although Redgrave was a 'walking Variorum', whose reading of all the play's famous textual cruces was masterly, he was too weighed down with all this apparatus criticus to scale the play's emotional heights.

I was in Paris the weekend that Tynan's notice appeared, and Michael had flown there to visit me. I bought the *Observer* at a news-stand on the Rue de Rivoli and we read it together in his hotel. We laughed a lot about the Cyclops, and that afternoon we went for a walk in Père Lachaise cemetery. It was the happiest afternoon I had ever spent with him. Failure or not – in fact it was light years from failure – I no longer felt responsible for his failures or successes.

Later that summer the painter Bryan Kneale came to Stratford to do a portrait of Michael's Hamlet which still hangs in the theatre's museum. Tynan and Kneale must have been in secret conference because the portrait, which to me seems hideous, totally confirms Tynan's image of a Cyclops, and not only that, but a monster in the last stages of hyperencephalopathy, a monster whose elephantine head rests on a pathetically attenuated trunk and spavined shanks. What prompted the museum's curator to stand by this truly monstrous piece of work baffled me. Perhaps it represented his and the artist's view (and Tynan's) of an intellectual actor.

Also that summer I heard that a Scandinavian (or perhaps it was a German) arts foundation had sent a theatre historian to Stratford. The person they sent had sat in the wings for every performance of my father's Hamlet, choreographing every move, every piece of business, composing in fact the portrait of a performance in progress which the painter had so failed to distil. I thought then, and I still think, it was a wonderful project, and alive or dead I would love to find the person who carried it out.

My father played in *Hamlet* seven times: three times as the Prince – at Cranleigh School; at the Old Vic (then the New Theatre) in 1950, a production which he also played in Kronborg Castle, Elsinore; and at Stratford in 1958; once as Horatio to Geoffrey Edwards's Hamlet at Liverpool Playhouse; once as Laertes to Olivier's Hamlet at the Old Vic in 1937; as Claudius in Olivier's inaugural production at the National Theatre (at the Old Vic) in 1963; and on television, as Polonius to Richard Chamberlain's Hamlet. There was nearly an eighth occasion. Peter Hall had promised him the Player King, but my father was ill, and the chance never actually presented itself. Yet in my mind's eye I imagine my father as the Player King watching Hamlet as he delivers his famous 'advice to the Players' –

> Speak the speech, I pray you, as I pronounced it to you, trippingly on the tongue; but if you mouth it, as many of your players do, I had as lief the town-crier spoke my lines . . .

I can imagine him nodding solemnly as Hamlet continues, solemnly because some of the advice is excellent common sense, but quizzically also because Hamlet is after all a rather spoilt amateur, and he, the Player King, is a professional, and frankly – here I can imagine my father's Player King raising his eyebrows to his fellow actors – what does some of Hamlet's advice mean? It is all very well, but what does 'in the very torrent, tempest, and, as I may say, whirlwind of your passion, you must acquire and beget a temperance that may give it smoothness' – what does it actually mean, practically speaking? Hamlet here sounds, and Shakespeare or his editor emphasises it with his stabbing punctuation, like a student who has spent too long in Wittenberg in endless metaphysical late-night discussions. Whereas the Player King, the professional, absorbs it all and says only, 'I warrant your honour', and then, after a further long piece of advice from Hamlet, says ironically: 'I hope we have reformed that indifferently with us, sir.'

But the challenge of the Player King – a problem which I suppose my father might have resolved beautifully – is that Shakespeare gives him a speech of fustian about Priam's death, a pastiche of Chapman or Greene, yet still requires the actor to weep real tears copiously, so that Hamlet can marvel afterwards

> that this player here,
> But in a fiction, in a dream of passion,
> Could force his soul so to his own conceit
> That from her working all his visage wanned;
> Tears in his eyes, distraction in his aspect . . .

My father would have done that as few other actors on earth. He discovered early in life that he could tap into whatever wellsprings of emotion produce real tears time and again at need. Many actors can cry on occasion, but he would cry for Hecuba, night after night.

There is also a ninth occasion I would mention briefly, even though it doesn't belong in this sequence because on this occasion he was in the audience. It was 1985, the month he died, and his granddaughter Natasha was playing Ophelia at the Young Vic, with Matthew Marsh as Hamlet, in David Thacker's production. Thacker admired Michael's work immensely, understood it and valued it; and the conjunction of the place, the time, the people involved and Natasha's Ophelia hangs in my memory.

Yet of all the occasions I would concentrate most upon his Hamlet at fifty. What, helpfully, can I remember of that performance? A stillness and a melancholy in the first scene; a directness about his soliloquies, such that he seemed to be both thinking aloud and, for the first time, talking to the audience as to a friend, but also observing always the line of the verse. Nevertheless I know these impressions, however much they mean to me, cannot adequately convey what I value to anyone who never saw him.

What I also remember – so clearly that it makes my hair stand on end even now – is the elemental force with which Hamlet breaks free from Horatio and Marcellus to pursue his father's ghost:

> My fate cries out,
> And makes each petty artery in this body
> As hardy as the Nemean lion's nerve.

'My fate cries out' was delivered with the full force of his lungs, literally at the top of his voice. It was something you could not recapture on any recording instrument because not even the most sophisticated modern equipment could take such a sudden crescendo, without the acoustic being adjusted. The sound engineer, knowing that it is about to come, will compensate in advance.

It seems to me that the whole drama of such a life as my father's and of my own relation to him is contained within the scene that follows. Most directors at that time followed Hamlet's idealised description of his father as the stern warrior king, Hyperion to his uncle's satyr. So it was in this production, where Hamlet's father's ghost was played by a fine classical actor, Anthony Nicholls. But it need not be so. Ingmar Bergman dressed the ghost in his nightshirt and the effect was harrowing. He was as I suppose Michael would be if I were to encounter him tomorrow in Balham High Road.

Which is preferable? It does not much matter. Both interpretations, no matter how contrary in appearance, can be true. What matters rather is that Hamlet convinces us that the man he is talking to really is his father, and in that Michael was supreme. Without doing anything, he conveyed the mounting horror of the son who learns from his father's mouth that his father was horribly murdered, and not only that, but that he suffered the most excruciating pain from the poison which his uncle used to murder him.

When Michael's own father died in Sydney in 1922, the only way Michael was aware of his death was that a telegram arrived at his stepfather's house, and that evening his mother and his stepfather went out for dinner to celebrate the fact that they could now get married.

One would not need to have read Freud's lectures on psychoanalysis – I don't think my father did, though I am not sure – and in particular his description in an army hospital in Vienna in 1917 of 'this famous Oedipus complex' to see how the Ghost's invocation to Hamlet was a brilliant imaginative verification of Michael's own experience as a boy:

> Ay, that incestuous, that adulterate beast
> With witchcraft of his wit, with traitorous gifts –
> O wicked wit, and gifts that have the power
> So to seduce! – won to his shameful lust
> The will of my most seeming-virtuous queen.
> O Hamlet, what a falling off was there,

> From me, whose love was of that dignity
> That it went hand in hand even with the vow
> I made to her in marriage; and to decline
> Upon a wretch whose natural gifts were poor
> To those of mine!

Andy's gifts may have been stirling. Indeed, if loyalty, generosity of a kind, patience up to a point – if these are virtues then Andy had them in abundance; while Roy, lascivious, intemperate Roy, was in reality far closer to the Claudius of Hamlet's fevered jealous imagination than to the royal Dane of his longing. But Michael's boyhood was founded on the belief that Andy had stolen his mother at that very time when he thought he had her to himself, and that in allowing this to happen his mother, who secretly communed with Roy in spiritualist seances, had thereby betrayed his real father and himself.

The ghost of Hamlet's father ends his frightful testimony as dawn is breaking by fading from Hamlet's sight. His last injunction is: 'Adieu, adieu, adieu! Remember me.'

How could Hamlet not remember this? His every waking moment until he has finally killed Claudius is tormented with the memory of his father.

> Remember thee?
> Ay, thou poor ghost, while memory holds a seat
> In this distracted globe.

None of this explains the power of my father's performance, though it may explain why this performance and this scene occupy so firm a place in my memory. That, unfortunately, is what all but the best criticism too easily settles for: the sensitivity of the critic.

13

The Mountebank's Tale

℘

I have on my sitting-room wall a poster advertising Roy's last performance at the Britannia Theatre in Hoxton. 'A Farewell Benefit for Mr Roy Redgrave', it says. He had played several seasons at the 'Brit', everything from Marcus Superbus in *The Sign of the Cross* to Hamlet – everything a leading man could play. He had been married there, to his first wife, Judith Kyrle. He must have been quite a favourite with the audiences, hence the farewell benefit. It was the kind of accolade, I suspect, which managements conferred only when they felt sure they would make sufficient profit from it to make the gesture worth while.

It was Roy's last performance in England. Before his second marriage, he had already spent two seasons in Australia as leading man to an American actress with the gloriously improbable name of Minnie Titell Brune, and he found the whole experience intoxicating. He revelled in the unaccustomed opportunities which come to the big fish in a small pond, and longed to repeat them. He persuaded a Mr Anderson to pay his passage and book him a season in Adelaide, Melbourne and Sydney.

Australia had a prosperous film industry. These were the days of early silent films, before Australian screens were colonised by American films, and my grandfather starred in several movies. But unfortunately I find it impossible in the few frames I have seen to distinguish his performance from the rest of the cast.

I did get to know him better, though, and I feel I can understand the kind of man and the kind of actor he was. On the way to starting work on my father's autobiography I sorted through a whole caseful of Roy's letters to my grandmother. I found that they fell neatly into two periods: their courtship, which lasted about three months, during which time my father was conceived; and a later period of about the same length, after Roy had sailed for Australia and before Daisy and Michael arrived there to join him. Not having the telephone to keep in touch with his wife and son he wrote almost every day, and after his own fashion, if not especially faithful, he seems at least to have been fond. But what makes his letters interesting to me is the portrait of Roy as an actor which emerges from them.

What made him choose acting as a career? What did he seek in the theatre, and what did he find? Such questions of course are never raised nor even glimpsed in his letters, yet they leave no doubt as to the answers. He acted for applause. The more, and the louder, the better. That does not mean that he did not discriminate, or that he always chose the shortest and easiest route to win his audience's approval. But applause nevertheless is what he wanted, more than anything else. If there are, in Michael Chekhov's definition, three kinds of actors, those who act for themselves, those who act for their fellow artists and those who act for the audience, Roy fell without question into the third category.

One could hardly blame him. He saw so little of his fellow artists by today's standards that it would have been hard, even if he had wanted to, for him to act for them. Nearing Adelaide he found himself unable to land for twenty-four hours because of rough weather – 'And when I did get off the boat I was seized by one of Anderson's men and a part of over 70 pages was thrust into my hands.' This was on Wednesday evening. He arrived in Melbourne by train, on Thursday morning, and there the newspapers had announced his first performance for Saturday night:

Practically two rehearsals for a part of 70-odd pages in a brand-new play, and with a company who had been rehearsing together for over a fortnight. Why on earth they didn't give me longer notice I can't make out, I can only suppose they relied on my quick study. Of course I made a fuss over it but what could I do? The bills were out and the opening boomed in all the papers. Besides, on the quiet, I wanted to get started soon as possible so as to avoid expenses of waiting around with two weeks' rehearsal.

He was to play Dave Goulburn in *The Man from Outback*. 'Bush dramas' they were called, a staple of Australian theatre. No expense was spared to build sets with sheep stations full of real sheep, mining villages, mountains, volcanoes and cataracts:

I am the title role, and my word I do lead a strenuous life. I roll down precipices extending from the flies to the footlights. I am locked up in a burning hut. Set upon by dogs. Released by my faithful horse – fights, shots, struggles galore – but enough decent stuff here and there which they allowed me to elaborate so as to make as artistic a show as possible.

The shortness of time to rehearse and learn the lines *was* troubling, but 'I got the stuff into my head by dint of sticking at it pretty nearly all day and night.' His efforts were rewarded: 'I wish you'd been there to hear my reception,' he wrote to Daisy. 'It was splendid. I had to bow and bow till I thought they'd never stop.'

Then comes a relapse. Roy seems to have shared with his son a tendency to fall suddenly and pathetically ill. That was bad enough, but it was made worse by the callous indifference of those around him to his illness:

Thursday and Friday I really thought I was dying. Perspiring at times so heavily as to soak the bed and then the next minute all shivering and shaking as though I had the ague. Racking pains in my head and so weak and helpless I could hardly raise my hand to my mouth. I daresay you can notice by my writing how shaky I am still. These beggars too, they don't seem to make any allowance. They seem to look upon it as something I've done on pur-

132

pose, just to spite them. They haven't been near me, except to send along my next part, 'Sherlock Holmes'.

There is no room for introspection in these letters, no self-doubt, no self-criticism. He is all of a piece, comfortable with himself, very much an actor of his time. He contrives his entrances so as to bring all the attention to himself. Even his exits are a little heightened, 'lifted', to leave no doubt that the scene is poorer by his absence. His final exit is exemplary. I have heard of actors, nearing death, whose concern was to find out what would be said in their obituaries, but none, I think, who took the same pains as Roy to write his own obituary. Among the letters which were passed to Michael by his mother was a cutting from the *Sydney Morning Herald*, headed, 'Roy Redgrave's Retrospect – Dead Actor's Last Lines':

Shortly before his death in a Sydney hospital on May 25th [1922], Roy Redgrave, the popular actor, wrote the following:

One of the best! Held his own 'in a crowd',
Lived like the rest (when finances allowed),
Slapped on the back as a jolly fine sport,
Drank any tack from bad whisky to port.
Fool to himself – that's the worst you can say;
Cruel to himself, for the health has to pay.
Months back he died, and we've only just heard
No friends by his side just to say the kind word.
No relatives near and no assets at all,
Quite lonely, I fear, when he answered the call.
One of the best. Held his own while he could.
Died like the rest, just when life seemed so good.

By the time Michael began to act, twelve years after his father's death, a thorough revolution had dethroned the Victorian and Edwardian actor-manager from his place of pre-eminence. It had been summoned by profound changes in taste and in the spirit of the times, and it had been carried out by directors, designers and writers – especially writers, and above all Shaw and Granville-Barker. No one remembers today the author of the play in which Sir Henry Irving made his greatest success, *The Bells*. In fact Irving's triumph rested on moments which were absolutely without words, as when Matthias hears in the far-off distance the sleigh-bells which tell him that the man he murdered has come back to haunt him.

Half a century after Irving, actors continued to have success in plays which no one expected would last beyond the season in which they appeared. None the less a revolution separates the star-vehicles of my grandfather's day, plays whose sole purpose was to heighten the personality of the leading performer, from the plays of a later period which, no matter how ephemeral, presupposed some kind of controlling influence, and some degree of commitment from director and cast which would permit the audience to see the play as a whole, and not merely by flashes of lightning. Even if in my time a further swing of the pendulum has tended to demote the writer, now and then, to not much more than the arranger of the actors' and director's improvisations, it has not yet fully restored the actor-manager, that familiar, alarming scarecrow of Victorian times. I doubt it ever will.

My father was almost thirty and had been three years on the stage when he made what was probably the most important single discovery of his professional life. Opposite the Victoria and Albert Museum was a bookshop specialising in theatre books and magazines, and it was while he was browsing there one afternoon that he discovered a copy of Stanislavsky's *An Actor Prepares*. He was appearing in a thoroughly ephemeral play called *A Ship Comes Home*. The author was Daisy Fisher, which sounds like a *nom de plume*. The leading lady was a popular actress called Mary Clare.

The effect of his discovery was startling and from Mary Clare's point of view thoroughly disconcerting. It was a matinee. He was playing a doctor and the set was the doctor's consulting-room. Looking at this set as it were for the first time he noticed that his stethoscope was hanging over the back of a chair, and all the contents of his surgical bag were scattered about his desk.

How untidy! he thought, and set about clearing away his paraphernalia. He had discovered, by accident, what sooner or later every student of Stanislavsky is bound to discover – the conflict of interest between what seems true and necessary to the individual actor, thinking of his or her role, and what is understood to be necessary and true to the scene and the play as a whole, by the actor who is trained to see his or her role as a part of a whole. It is a conflict which many disciples of Stanislavsky never resolve, or resolve piecemeal, or resolve falsely by elevating the truth of the individual character to an absolute.

> Josef Charles [my father wrote] was a classical actor in the unusual but real sense of the word. He never altered the balance of the part, consciously or unconsciously, to suit his own style or personality. He scrupulously measured each part in relation to the text and the author's meaning.

Josef Charles is the hero of *The Mountebank's Tale*, my father's only published novel, and so far as I know his only original work of fiction. It was written during his last season at Stratford in 1958, the season of *Hamlet* and *Much Ado About Nothing*. Every summer the theatre was host to a series of lectures on Shakespeare, by scholars and critics and occasionally by actors. My father was invited to contribute, as he had in previous seasons.

His four Rockefeller Lectures at Bristol University had been published. So too had a miscellany of lectures and articles, under the title *Mask or Face*. I do not know what subject was proposed on this occasion, nor why he decided to depart so far from his brief. Probably he would have said that he had nothing at that moment to say on the subject of theatre without risk of repeating himself. But I think rather the opposite. Whether he realised it or not he had so much to say, so much of an urgent and pressing kind, that he needed the cover of fiction to say it.

Whatever the reason, the lecture which he wrote, in about three days, and delivered in the old conference room at Stratford, now the Swan Theatre, was not a lecture in form but a work of fiction. *The Times* reported that his audience gave it rapt attention, though 'one felt that for such a performer they would have given almost as much attention to a reading of the telephone directory.' *The Mountebank's Tale*, even in its published form, was no more than a long short story of 130 pages. I suppose the version my father read in lieu of a lecture at Stratford was even shorter; but I can well imagine that his audience was entertained, and even enthralled.

The narrator is a successful famous actor of the English theatre, and we meet him in his club, which is very like the Garrick. He is given a photograph of two men. One figure he recognises as that of a late friend, a writer and theatre historian. The other he cannot immediately identify, but from the setting, with its exotic juxtaposition of a seventeenth-century Cotswold farmhouse and giant eucalyptus trees, he deduces that the photograph was taken in California, and he guesses that the second face belongs to a legendary Austrian actor, retired in Hollywood, Josef Charles.

My father was a friend and admirer of the Danish writer Isak Dinesen, and from her Gothic tales he acquired the trick of building his introduction, to heighten the suspense and anticipation for what follows. He also stresses cleverly the likeness of the narrator to himself, to deflect attention from the fact, which only struck me on a later reading, that the real subject of the story – namely, the Viennese actor Josef Charles – is himself.

It is the story of an actor and his double. The actor is a supremely gifted, cultivated, classical actor. His double is a young Englishman some ten years his junior but identical to himself in every outward respect. The actor has taught the younger man German, and has also taught him how to act. In so doing he finds that his young pupil has a natural gift almost the equal of his own.

Charles is preparing to appear in a Viennese light comedy, the plot of which relies on a pair of identical twins. The play has been written for a virtuoso, Charles himself, to double both twins, but for a prank he decides to allow his protégé to play the other twin. The audience is delighted with the substitution, and for a while the young actor basks in the delicious warmth of their applause.

He is allowed no other parts in his master's repertoire, however, and after a while he starts to pine for independence and the chance to make his own career out of the shadow of his great master. Seeing this the older actor decides on an even more daring substitution. In another one-act comedy about an old man and his valet he allows his protégé to take his part as the old man, while he disguises himself in the supporting role of the valet.

The audience now is unaware of the substitution. They applaud the old man to the echo, believing him to be played by their idol. The young actor, emboldened by their applause, becomes more adventurous, inventing and improvising new bits of comic business. Josef Charles, on the other hand, as the valet, does something the young man has never seen him do before: he forgets his lines.

Soon after that performance Josef Charles disappears, on the eve of what should have been the climax of his international career, a tour of America. And now the young man takes his place, first on the tour, later in Hollywood. He becomes Josef Charles. He is the 'mountebank' of the title.

The story is an elaborate construction of Chinese boxes, of mirrors and illusions, of 'Now you see it, now you don't'. The reader is never sure until the end whether the old actor in Hollywood is Josef Charles himself or Charles's double, as the actor claims. The story is full of interest as a tale told by an actor about acting. Yet for me it has an added interest: behind all the disguises, inventions and subterfuges I constantly glimpse my father, beckoning me on, telling me, 'This is why I act, this is what I am.'

The crux lies in the ambiguous relationship of the great actor to his double. The first is a 'classical artist' in the purest sense of the word. The other is his twin in appearance, his equal in talent, but his opposite in temperament. Josef Charles has every gift but one: he lacks the gift of showmanship. Beside his alter ego, who owes everything he knows to his master's training, Josef Charles nevertheless feels impoverished. As the younger actor puts it:

> Josef had every quality of greatness except that one. That he could not ever learn because he did not wish to learn it ... I did not have to learn it. It was always part of my nature. I was a born mountebank. When I caused him to forget his lines in that little comedy it was because I did things which he, with his fastidious taste, did not exactly refuse to do. Quite simply, it would never have occurred to him to do them.

I said that my father was Josef Charles, and it is true that often when he is describing Charles he is speaking of himself. This description of a dress rehearsal, for instance, is taken moment by moment from a dress rehearsal of *Antony and Cleopatra* which I myself witnessed, with mounting fear and disbelief, as a boy of thirteen:

> The dress rehearsal was a disaster. I could swear that he had not forgotten his lines. He could have said them in his sleep. But the slightest detail of lighting or a costume worn by some other player was enough to make him dry up. Then he would insist on going back again and again but the more he tried the more spontaneity deserted him. There were flashes of technical brilliance but his heart was not in it. His face even seemed drained of personality, his eyes dull and he even seemed to be having trouble with his gloriously strong and variable voice.

Like Charles, my father was intensely self-critical and intensely fastidious. Like Charles too he complained, but secretly in his diaries, that he lacked the instinct of a showman. Side by side with his great contemporary Olivier he was, at his best, as in *Uncle Vanya*, much the better artist. But if for some reason he felt ill at ease with his materials he suffered, and knew he suffered by comparison; then he envied Olivier his showmanship, and wished it for himself.

Yet he was also Josef Charles's double, just as he was also his father's son. He was both actor and double, artist and showman, mask and face, and as often as not these two contradictory sides to his talent were at war.

The most telling, and also the most personal, passage in the novel is a description of a nightmare in which the mask slips, a nightmare in which all pretence, all illusion, is stripped away and he is left naked. This time it is the double who is speaking, but I know that it is also my father, because this was his recurring nightmare:

It was hot, unbearably hot, in my dressing-room. My hands trembled as I applied my make-up and the grease-paint would not stay in place, but would slide around my face and into my ears and hair like drops of oil on a pond. I had the dresser turn on electric fans all round the make-up table and sat; shivering while I applied chalk-dry sticks of grease to my pinched features. I could hear Josef's voice still. He was shouting my cue to enter, over and over again. *I'm coming!* I screamed, but no sound came from my lips. At last the make-up was done. I rose from the table and reached for my shirt. As I did so the electric fans stopped and instantly I started to sweat again. I looked in dismay at the mirror and there I could see the make-up slowly start to drain down my face, over my chin, down my neck and on to my chest. When the grease-paint reached this point it recomposed itself and there, amid the hairs on my chest, was the grease-paint portrait of my face. I stared at it in horror. I wanted to run on stage to show him that it was not my fault if I was late, that I had done my make-up, but that it would not stay in place. My legs would not move. I started to cry and, reflected in the mirror, I could see my tears running down, down from my bleared eyes to the grease-paint caricature below.

14

Losing and Finding

⚘

One more quotation, from the same source. Josef Charles is talking to his double:

> 'How stupid you are, Paul. Have you never realised that I have no ambition. What drives me is not ambition.'
> 'What is it then?'
> 'A quest.'
> 'A quest for what?'
> 'Perhaps it is not a quest. Indeed I sometimes think of it as a flight.'
> 'A flight from what?'
> 'From what else but myself.'

Again I feel sure that in this exchange, with its insistent litany – like the child's game 'Knock knock ... Who's there?' – Michael is speaking of himself. Idealised, no doubt; purged and purified perhaps – because of course he was by no means without ambition. But ambition was never his spur.

A flight from himself? There is a note, at the end of an early diary, which speaks of 'losing' and 'finding' himself. It is headed 'The artist as "man of character"':

> It has been said that the two are incompatible. This agrees with the theory of the artistic temperament as a disease. Particularly it is true of actors, whose nature demands that they should lose themselves, or rather find themselves, in other characters. The extent to which characterisation alters my private life is frightening

and at times ridiculous. To live happily it would seem that I must concentrate on the portrayal of romantic, upright, simple men, which anyway, next to the childishness of Tusenbach or Sir Andrew, is what I do best.

I don't know what specific circumstances may have prompted my father to write this. It is on the last page of the diary which describes his affair with 'T' at the beginning of the war, the same diary in which he often quotes from André Gide. Perhaps a little of Gide's sententiousness has rubbed off on him.

His handwriting is usually neat and legible, but it wavers disjointedly towards the end of this paragraph as though he were very tired, or a little drunk; or in distress. After Tusenbach in *Three Sisters* and Sir Andrew Aguecheek he had played Lord Harry Monchensey in the first production of T. S. Eliot's *The Family Reunion*, and I suspect it is this part which he complains has a 'frightening and at times ridiculous' effect on his private life. He was troubled by the ambivalence he found in Eliot's poetry, but especially by the contrast between the admiration we feel for Orestes and Electra in the drama of the *Oresteia* and the fact that in everyday life we condemn such feelings and actions as morbid, pathological and of course criminal.

Actors often speak of losing themselves in a part. Most actors experience, once or twice, that moment in which their character 'takes over'. It is exhilarating, even a little frightening, the more so if the actor were to lose himself not for a moment or two but for a whole evening. It is more alarming still if he finds that the character who has taken over in performance is starting to invade his private life.

Probably a little more exhibitionism would have helped to keep this fear in check. And there was exhibitionism in my father certainly, as there is in every artist, more or less. But in that contract with himself which every actor makes my father struck a hard bargain. He came to terms early on with his exhibitionism and he kept to those terms scrupulously for the rest of his life. He never renegotiated the contract. There was never any of that provocative display which makes an audience want to interrupt a performance with applause and cheers. As the play went on, the audience would fall under the spell of a chaste, invisible baton. At the end they would applaud slowly at first, as if half awake from a dream.

When I try to recollect his work as a whole I see many exceptions to these 'romantic, upright, simple men' at which he excelled. In pursuit of such exceptions I would cite his performance as the ventriloquist possessed by his dummy in the 1945 film *Dead of Night*. Most of all I would mention his performance as Crocker Harris, the classics master, in the film *The Browning Version*, released in 1951. I would put that performance alongside the work of my favourite cinema actors, Michael Simon and Louis Jouvet.

For the first few moments my father's high, dry, nasal voice, slowly, wearily, as if for the thousandth time, construing a piece of Greek verse, strikes me as absurd, impossible. I want to call out, 'Don't! You can't possibly sustain it!' I remember having much the same response to another great screen actor, Marlon Brando, when he boards the *Bounty* as Fletcher Christian and turns to speak to Bligh in the accents of a Regency fop.

Everything about my father's performance in those first few frames gives me anguish: the tips of his fingers placed together under his chin; his stooping walk; the flick of his eyes to a remote corner of the classroom in case he might detect some inattention, some laughter. It seems such a high-wire performance, demanding that the audience accept it entirely on its own terms. And it has no safety net.

Yet I do accept it, entirely, after the first few moments. And I realise that in this instance too the process is one of losing and finding. In Rattigan's story the schoolmaster Crocker Harris had been just such a romantic, simple, upright man at the start of his career, but to protect himself from chaos, and to screen himself from what might happen if any of his pupils were to reveal for him the affection he feels for them, he has adopted a mask of pedantry and ruthless discipline. With this mask he has alienated generations of boys, and alienated himself, becoming known as 'The Himmler of the Lower Fifth'.

A more good-natured and more understanding audience now sees in Rattigan's work an analogue for his own condition, whereas a generation ago no one saw anything but middle-class, middlebrow, thoroughly predictable well-made plays. I confess I do find Rattigan predictable; but I think there is nothing impertinent – quite the contrary – in a deconstruction of his plays which would reveal the deceptions and evasions that were forced on many men who were gay.

At the climax of the story one of the boys gives Crocker Harris, as a present, a copy of Browning's translation of Aeschylus' *Agamemnon*. On the flyleaf he has written an inscription: 'God looks kindly on a gentle master.' The effect on Crocker Harris is one of terrifying catharsis. His body starts to shake, he turns away from the boy and he sends him out of the room before giving way to uncontrollable grief.

It is impossible for me to witness that scene now without recalling the evening I spent with Michael in 1967 after Luke was born. I am not suggesting that any such parallel would have occurred to Michael. The scene from Rattigan was filmed many years before the scene we played together in real life. Moreover, I know that, even had they not been so far apart, my father would have avoided drawing directly on his own emotional experience to fashion Crocker Harris. He was too conscious an artist to seek that kind of short cut. And when life sometimes seemed to imitate art too closely he was made uncomfortable by it.

Even so, I have come to realise, painfully, that all drama, even Shakespeare's, is a form of autobiography. So is acting. In the three films which my father made with the director Anthony Asquith, the romantic, simple, upright man appears at least twice. *The Way to the Stars*, which was shot in a deserted RAF camp near Catterick just before the end of the war, is full of such types. David Archdale, my father's character, dies early in the story, even though Michael has the starring role. I bought it, not long ago, as a video film, and was surprised to find that the script for this film also is by Terence Rattigan. It is full of the kind of slang which at first makes you wince, rather as Michael's accent does at the start of *The Browning Version*. An aeroplane doesn't crash, it 'prangs'. A 'chap' doesn't die, he has 'bought it'. My father plays an airman who is also a poet, which is all right and perfectly English as long as one clears one's throat and confesses that one is not much good oneself at understanding 'that sort of thing'.

Rattigan used real verses by a real poet, John Pudney, whose poetry is so transparently clear and simple that not even the most amiable British duffer could pretend not to understand it.

> Do not despair
> For Johnny Head-in-air
> He sleeps as sound
> As Johnny underground
>
> Better by far
> For Johnny-the-Bright-Star
> To keep your head
> And see his children fed.

My father's voice repeats these lines in the last moments of the film. I am sure he was right to feel in them a strong socialist undercurrent. The belief that all the children of all the Johnnies should be fed, clothed and taught was very strong, and it was that which brought the Labour government in on a landslide in the year the film was released.

The Importance of Being Earnest, the last of the three films he made with Asquith, is also about a romantic, simple man, John Worthing, though he is not entirely upright because to win the hand of Gwendolyn Fairfax he must humour her by pretending that his name is Ernest. However, the virtues of romance and simplicity conquer in the end and he is proved to have been truthful and upright too because his name really was Ernest.

I can think of other exceptions to those romantic, simple, upright men whom my father played so well. In fact not one of his Shakespearian parts accords with that description, or with Sir Andrew Aguecheek's childishness. But I think the phrase entirely appropriate for Uncle Vanya, which was my favourite of the parts he played, and perhaps his too. I know he felt proud of his performance as Vanya, which was perhaps not so unusual, and that he went out of his way to ensure that I would see it. That was very unusual.

It was 1962 and I was playing in London. To make sure that I could get back from his matinee at Chichester in time for my own evening performance he had a taxi wait for me at the Festival Theatre stage door to whisk me at top speed to the station. Even so I was only back in my theatre, the Vaudeville, with moments to spare.

As Vanya he did not seem to characterise, in the sense that he borrowed no external traits of speech or bearing. He simply used his own physical attributes, his height, his voice and a puzzled, slightly clouded expression which his face often wore, and with the most delicate shifts of emphasis he reassembled them in a portrait which said 'I am Vanya'. As is often the case with very good acting, he did not have to work to convince the audience, because he had convinced himself. In fact, to be pedantic, I don't think he even had to do that. He simply accepted he was Vanya. He had only to add the 'childishness' which he found in Tusenbach and Aguecheek – sufficient childishness to explain why Vanya, no matter how deeply in love, is never likely to marry; sufficient for him to aim a pistol at his rival's head, and miss; sufficient also never to lose all hope that there will be a better tomorrow.

Of this production the theatre critic Michael Billington wrote:

To see Olivier and Redgrave sharing the stage with such total unselfishness and joyfully clasping their hands together in blessed union at the curtain call was an uplifting, hopeful experience. One was reminded of the singular fact that Britain's four or five greatest actors have always been on the friendliest personal terms and shown scarcely a glimmer of professional jealousy: a far cry from the often poisonous rivalries of great actors in the eighteenth and nineteenth centuries.

It is true. I think my father was as happy in those two seasons at Chichester as he had ever been – happy to be sharing the stage with Olivier, and happy to look forward to the opening of the National Theatre, which he was to share with Olivier, at the Old Vic. Of all the actors of his generation he had most consistently championed the idea of a national theatre.

There are many stories of Olivier's cruelty to other actors. They suggest that no matter how confident he was, and had reason to be, in his own supremacy, he resented any success that came too near his own. Probably these stories are exaggerated, and perhaps a great many are apocryphal. But I know that for years I nursed a brooding hatred of Olivier for what I felt sure was his destruction of my father's confidence at the National Theatre.

I was away in America when the first production opened in 1963. Olivier directed my father, as Claudius, in *Hamlet*. Knowing how much this must have meant to him I was almost as anxious for him as I had been when I was a boy, but I could get no clear idea of his performance from reviews, or from the accounts of friends who had seen it. By the time I came back to Britain the production was no longer in the repertoire.

Whatever uneasiness he felt was magnified ten times for his next production, as Hobson in *Hobson's Choice*. He couldn't remember the lines, nor get the Salford accent he was trying for. My mind went back to that nightmarish dress rehearsal of *Antony and Cleopatra* in 1953 when he had dried on every speech, and didn't always seem to know which scene he was in; I couldn't bring myself to see him. Like *Hamlet*, the production was soon withdrawn.

I did see his final appearance at the Old Vic, as Solness in Ibsen's *The Master Builder* in 1964. I knew he was having great difficulty with it, and I wrote to him when the production

"Worth Their Weight in Gold"

Dear Sirs,—Your Yeast-Vite Tablets have been a wonderful pick-me-up. I was always bad with nervous and suffering from severe headaches every day. Since I started Yeast-Vite I never felt better in my life, they are worth their weight in gold. Thanking you, Sirs, for this wonderful Tonic. Yours faithfully, Mrs J. G.

Yeast-Vite brand tablets bring quick relief from Headaches, Nerves, Lassitude, Depression, Insomnia, Rheumatism, Indigestion, etc. Sold everywhere at 7d., 1/1, 3/5 and 5/8 including purchase tax.

T IN EACE

SILENCE ON THE MOSCOW RADIO GERMAN AND

—ment deem it neces—

—the Soviet Govern—are the view of the —ernment as to the —her attitude in this —s attitude, indepen—ather the Bulgarian —ishes it, leads not to —on of peace, but to an —e sphere of war and —of Bulgaria in war ;

—y, the Soviet Govern—s peace policy, is not —render any support —e Bulgarian Govern—cution of her present

—et Government finds —o make this state—rly in view of un—urs spread in the —ess which funda—present the real atti—et Government.' "

—y be an —arning

—nnouncements from

Germany, since it —l extend the war. —Kremlin's excuse for a —sympathy is the most

MICHAEL REDGRAVE
"I declined to write any such letter."

Italians Raid Quake Town Again

While Greece yesterday called on the world to judge the "unforgettable atrocity" of the Italians in bombing earthquake-stricken Larissa, the Duce's bombers raided the town again.

Expressing the fierce anger of the nation over the first raid, the Press says : "Scarcely 24 hours after the terrible earthquake shocks had partly destroyed the town the Italian bombers arrived bent upon finishing the destruction and massacring the population, who had nothing to shelter them but improvised tents.

"This unforgettable atrocity demonstrates that among Italian airmen and their General Staff is to be found a degree of barbarity almost without precedent."—Reuter.

B.B.C. Gives Stars An Ultimatum

"QUIT PEOPLE'S CONVENTION, OR YOU DON'T BROADCAST"

MICHAEL REDGRAVE, THE STAGE AND FILM STAR, AND MORE THAN A DOZEN OTHER WELL-KNOWN ACTORS, ACTRESSES, PRODUCERS AND MUSICIANS HAVE BEEN INFORMED BY THE B.B.C. THAT UNLESS THEY STATE IN WRITING THAT THEY WITHDRAW THEIR SUPPORT OF THE PEOPLE'S CONVENTION THEY WILL NOT BE ALLOWED TO BROADCAST AGAIN.

They were given a week in which to think it over. The facts have been reported to Equity and the Musicians' Union and are to be raised in Parliament.

A special committee of which Beatrix Lehmann, the actress, and Walter Hudd, who is now playing in "Thunder Rock" at the St. Martin's Theatre, are members, has been set up by the National Council for Civil Liberties to fight the ban.

"None of Your Business"

Mr. Redgrave told the News Chronicle yesterday that a week ago he received a letter from the B.B.C. asking him to call to discuss an important matter.

"I was interviewed by a B.B.C. solicitor and an executive," he said. "They told me that the Governors of the B.B.C. had decided that those who supported the People's Convention should not be employed.

"They asked me if I would write a letter to the organisers of the Convention withdrawing my support and send a copy to the B.B.C. I replied that my personal views were none of their business and that I did not propose to discuss the matter any further. Of course, I declined to write any such letter.

"I asked them directly if this meant that I should not receive another B.B.C. contract and they replied that this was so.

Will Support Anti-Ban Committee

"I reminded them that I was broadcasting on the following Sunday and they said this would be in order. I hope my singing last night didn't do the country

INVASION PORTS BOMBED

INVASION ports on the French coast were heavily attacked by R.A.F. bombers last night.

Watchers on the Kent coast saw brilliant flashes light up the sky above Calais and Boulogne.

Scores of searchlights were in action and German ground defences offered lively resistance, spraying the sky with star-shells and streams of flaming onions.

BREST ATTACKED

Docks at Brest from which enemy surface raiders and submarines attack shipping in the Atlantic were heavily bombed for nearly two hours on Sunday night.

Many sticks of bombs burst about the dry dock where a German cruiser of the Hipper class is lying.

Darlan-Laval Talks Today

Admiral Darlan will lunch with Laval when he arrives in Paris today for new talks, states the German official news agency in Berlin.

Marshal Pétain's representative in Paris, Count Fernand de Brinon, will be their host at luncheon, the Berlin radio announces.

Today's visit will be Darlan's fifth to Paris since Christmas. His journeys have dealt with problems of Franco-German cooperation.

The German-controlled Press in Paris is still dissatisfied with the subservience of the Vichy Government.—Reuter and B.U.P.

British Trawler Sunk

The British trawler Ouse (Lieut.-Commander J. E. Grice, R.N.) has been sunk, the Admiralty announced last night.

GREEKS DESTROY ITALIAN PLANES

Last night's Greek communiqué said : "Action by small infantry detachments. Intensive and successful artillery activity. Our air force has shot down two enemy aircraft. No damage was done to our aircraft.—Reuter.

LONDON BLACK-OUT

7.15 p.m.—7.8 a.m.

BEST

LEFT *News Chronicle* headline, 4 March 1941

BELOW MR in the Royal Navy, front row, centre, 1941

ABOVE MR and Vanessa at Bedford House, late 1940s, author sitting on steps

ABOVE RIGHT MR and Lynn, 1940s

RIGHT MR with author, 1940s

OPPOSITE The family at Bedford House, 1946

MR as Macbeth, Aldwych Theatre, 1947

ABOVE Bryan Kneale's portrait of MR as Hamlet, Stratford-upon-Avon, 1958

LEFT MR as Antony and Peggy Ashcroft as Cleopatra in *Antony and Cleopatra* in rehearsal at the Prince's Theatre, 1953

TOP MR, Nancy Coleman, Kirk Douglas and
Katina Paxinou in *Mourning Becomes
Electra*, for which MR received an Oscar
nomination, 1951

ABOVE MR with Brian Smith in *The Browning
Version*, 1950, for which he won the prize for
best actor at the Cannes Film Festival, the first
English actor to do so

RIGHT MR as King Lear, Stratford-upon-Avon, 1953

ABOVE MR as Hamlet, Stratford-upon-Avon, 1958

ABOVE RIGHT MR at Angkor Thom, Cambodia, a break from shooting *The Quiet American* in Saigon, 1957

RIGHT Moscow tour, 1958–9. Angela Baddeley, MR, Dorothy Tutin, tour guide, Coral Browne, Rachel Kempson and Geraldine McEwan

TOP **MR** and Vanessa

CENTRE **MR** and the author

BOTTOM The family at MR's funeral, March 1985

As King Lear, with Vanessa, at the Roundhouse in London, 1982

was on tour in Newcastle, trying to inspire him with my confidence that he would find in Solness what he was looking for. He wrote back saying that, yes, he felt he did understand Solness and *could* play him. It was a characteristically diffident and self-deprecating letter, but in this context it seemed not to augur well.

I cannot remember anything of his performance. My anxiety and the sadness I felt for him has obliterated all trace of it from my memory.

It is strange now to read other people's memories of that season, and to see how much they found to praise in him, whether as the tyrannical father in *Hobson's Choice*, or in Ibsen. I can hardly bear to think of that time because I know that for him it represented a crushing, bruising experience. And perhaps because I had no other explanation I laid the fault for much of that on Olivier.

I think differently now. I imagine that Olivier was almost as baffled by his friend's unhappiness as he was himself. And I know too that any attempt to help my father at such a time, clumsy or sensitive, well meant or otherwise, would as likely as not have only deepened his sense of insecurity. Olivier certainly made such attempts. He suggested that perhaps it would lighten the burden of responsibility on Michael if he, Olivier, took over one or two of his parts. My father, of course, declined the offer, and felt trebly insecure, in the belief that Olivier wanted to be rid of him. It must have confirmed all his worst fears when, soon after his departure from the National Theatre, Olivier did in fact take over the part of Solness and made a success of it with a performance quite different from Michael's.

I brooded over this for years; but I realise now that it was quite beside the point. Slowly, very slowly at first, because it did not become obvious in him until middle age, Parkinson's disease was affecting his brain. The damage as yet was very slight, and far too little for diagnosis, but its effects were already noticeable and, because there was no explanation or diagnosis, they were all the more disturbing.

A physician examining my father at that time had a difficult diagnosis to make. There were so many possible explanations for his symptoms, and some were familiar and reassuring. What he could not do then was to see inside my father's brain, using magnetic resonance imaging, to detect those areas where the blood flow was impaired, or to see the build of neurofibrillary tangles which are characteristic of the illness. The technique known as frequency shifted burst imaging allows the whole brain to be imaged with good resolution in less than two seconds, without using radioactive isotopes. It wasn't available for many years after the onset of my father's illness. It is available now, though very few patients have access to it.

It was April 1983 when we finished my father's autobiography. Wilks Water, my mother's cottage in the wood in Hampshire, was up for sale. They had decided to move to London, and were searching for a house or a flat somewhere near my elder sister's.

The catalpa tree, which saves its splendour until every other tree is green, and loses it before all the rest, was not yet in leaf, but every other bush or shrub was in bloom. My father had grown a long white beard. He seemed to relish the prospect of living once again in London. Just so he greeted that brilliant photographer Jane Bown who came to take a picture of him on his seventy-fifty birthday.

> Thou hast nor youth, nor age,
> But, as it were, an after-dinner's sleep,
> Dreaming on both

says the Duke in *Measure for Measure*, trying to reconcile young Claudio to the sentence of death which Angelo has pronounced on him.

Michael dictated his last chapter, only two pages long, without any help or prompting from me. It is a kind of after-dinner dozing dream in which his mother and his aunt Mabel are gossiping together, and he is hovering over the scene, a presiding ghost, one moment a child, the next an old man. But when he came to the Duke's lines he stopped and checked himself in mid-flight.

'Is that right?' he asked me.

'Yes, absolutely.'

'Are you sure?'

'Word for word, absolutely right.'

'That's not what I mean. I know I've quoted it right. What I mean is . . . is it right?'

'I don't understand.'

'I mean is Shakespeare right? Is that how it is?'

'You should know.'

'Why should I know?'

I felt reproved. And so I should have been; for of course we tease ourselves in childhood with the hope that we shall understand more as we grow older, and in adult life we look forward to the wisdom which is promised us with advancing years, and all our life we are advancing hopefully towards a maturity which never comes. So, yes, I could well understand why Michael, who now spent so much of his day asleep, or dozing, as if conserving his energy for a sudden burst of activity, might nevertheless question what the Duke says, although the Duke's words seemed to me, from my vantage point, to apply with uncanny accuracy to my father's condition.

'Well, how does it feel?' I asked him.

'I don't feel old,' he said. 'I just feel slow.'

The Jesuit dialectician who first noted that the child is father to the man enunciated an even more profound truth than he knew. For the truth is not simply that we are our childhood, but that we as children feel responsible for our parents. If we are not careful we become the parents to our parents. We try to solve their problems, and we go on trying to solve them, even after they have died. The contradiction is particularly acute in my father's case. He never knew his real father, and felt himself an orphan. By the end I came to stand, in relation to him, *in loco parentis*.

My father-in-law, David Markham, died in December 1983. I loved him very much as a fine, courageous man, physically the most beautiful and handsome man I ever saw. His death made me realise what I had refused to face until then, that Michael was extremely ill and might soon die. With Kika I began to visit him more frequently. It was the happiest time of our lives together. I could sit for hours at a time with him, often saying little or nothing.

It hurts me still to remember him, and although in occasional sly moments I feel that I shall never get over his death, I know that in truth I have got over it, and have more or less let him go. I can become, late though it is, his son.

Much of that is thanks to David Markham; but much also is thanks to my father. On the face of it he declined into ill health, while his greatest contemporaries continued in full vigour. Illness unfairly robbed him of the last chapters of his working life, and one result was that critics and theatre historians, whose memories are short, often leave him out of account when they write about his time.

Unseen by them, however, my father began a new career. He could no longer learn a new part, but his long-term memory for the parts he had already played was almost unimpaired. With the director Alan Strachan and his friends Rosalind Shanks and David Dodimead he devised *Shakespeare's People*, an anthology of Shakespeare to tour around the world.

His voice was much quieter than it had been, but still very expressive. His movements were awkward, rather stiff and hesitant. But with the extra adrenalin which a performance before an audience stimulates his actions became more fluent and his voice more firm. He would sleep on the coach by day and come awake at night. In many of the towns and cities he visited there would be parties or receptions in his honour and often, I imagine, he would need help to find his bed.

That is where his autobiography ended, apart from the short, dream-like epilogue. Touring from town to town, from hotel to hotel, living out of a suitcase. Like a sailor, happy that he has a wife and children waiting for him at the end of his voyage, but in no hurry to come home. Reunited with his ancestors, Redgraves, Scudamores, Ellsworthys, all of whom lived and died as touring actors.

He told me about his aunt Mabel, who in palmier days had played Josephine in London to her husband's Napoleon. He last saw her when he was a student at Cambridge. He had bicycled over to find her and her new husband in the village hall, at Saffron Walden, selling the tickets at the box office before darting backstage to reappear before the footlights in a play called *The Woman Always Pays*. As he watched the play he was struck by its similarity to a much better-known play, *Hindle Wakes*. The characters' names were different but in every other respect it was the same.

'It's very similar to *Hindle Wakes*,' he told Mabel, after the show.

'Isn't it just?' she said. 'Glad you spotted that. As a matter of fact it *is Hindle Wakes*.'

'So why did you call it . . . ?'

'Had to, didn't we? Couldn't afford the royalties.'

It seemed a self-defeating economy, considering there were only seven people in the audience, but she was pleased with it.

For almost three years we worked on his autobiography, and during that time I became more at home and at ease with him. I began to respect him also for his sheer bravery, and as time went on my respect grew. I never heard him complain. In all the discomfort of his long-drawn-out illness he never once uttered a syllable of self-pity. Parkinson's inflicts countless small humiliations on its patients, but he bore them all with stoic dignity.

He would lock himself in every lavatory he entered, despite my entreaties to leave the door unlocked. I was afraid that his fingers, although still strong enough to slide or turn a bolt shut, would be too weak to open it, and I was right.

'I've locked myself in, I'm afraid.'

'Why did you lock it? I asked you not to.'

'I was afraid someone would come in.'

'Wouldn't it be better if they could?' I complained wearily as I tried to scale the lavatory wall. It was never easy. It also looked, to the casual observer who often caught me in the act of toppling over the partition on to my father, faintly criminal.

Stoicism, says the *Dictionary of Classical Literature*, began with Zeno in Cyprus. It preached the universal brotherhood of man, without distinction between Greek and barbarian, free-man and slave. Its doctrine was the duty of universal benevolence and justice. Most of that is compatible with my father's outlook and demeanour. He had begun his working life as a fervent socialist, and though he never recovered his fervour he never lost his principles.

Only later, according to my source, in its systematisation by Zeno's disciples, did Stoicism come to signify the withdrawal from life and the world which we usually associate with the term, like Viola's imaginary sister who sat 'like Patience on a monument / Smiling at grief'. I do not think of my father as unworldly; quite the contrary. But I have never seen or heard of anyone who confronted illness and death so calmly and cheerfully. A religious zealot may greet death with a smile believing he is about to meet God. My father had no such illusion. He never wavered in his materialist belief that this life is the only life we have, and though he looked sympathetically on those whose religion promises them an afterlife he never wanted to share it.

I know my mother misses him. She had sacrificed so much of her career to his, and to us as children. But even before he became ill her career had begun to bloom again, and she was playing leading parts on television and in the theatre. After the beginning of his illness she became the only breadwinner. She looked after him throughout his illness, with all the wear and tear on the spirit which caring of that kind causes. Yet all her finest achievements as an actress came at this time. As a boy I used to predict to her that her best time would come, and it turned out I was right. As 'Kate the Good Neighbour' for the BBC and as Lady Manners in *Jewel in the Crown* she created two unforgettable characters. She played Volumnia to my Coriolanus at the Young Vic in 1989. Her blazing pride and joy when she greeted me after the victory at Corioli stopped me in my tracks every night.

Had Michael lived a few more months my mother and he would have been married for fifty years. I still cannot resolve whether that is good or bad. I know my mother suffered very much at times, and there were occasions when I felt like begging her to part with him because I was convinced she would have led a happier life if she had been independent. When I see how many times in their early life he came home after a night out to find her anxious and in tears I want even now to curse him. But I know my mother has no inclination to complain. One of her favourite Shakespearian quotations is Richard II's rebuke to Thomas Mowbray:

> It boots thee not to be compassionate;
> After our sentence, 'plaining comes too late.

And she had lived her life by it.

She knew, and was good friends with, almost all Michael's loves, just as he knew and was friends with hers. In her autobiography, *A Family and its Fortunes*, she writes with great affection of an evening spent with Noël Coward some time in the early 1970s:

> That evening Noël said to me: 'I have loved Michael, but he is very difficult, and you must have had your difficulties.'
>
> I told him that in fact he, Noël, had upset me greatly one night at the beginning of the war. It was the last night before Michael went to Plymouth, to join up. I had wanted to spend the evening with Michael, but he had spent it instead with Noël.
>
> Noël said that he hadn't wished to hurt me, and that it was no use having regrets about what you have done, but he had found Michael so irresistibly charming. I couldn't but agree with him.

I know my sisters miss him. For Vanessa he was much the most important influence upon her life as an artist, and his work the best that acting can aspire to. As for Michael, he worshipped Vanessa's talent as if it had nothing to do with his own, and yet was always very watchful and objective. Lynn, whom he neglected as a child and of whom he expected nothing, grew up to astonish him in a way neither Vanessa nor I ever could.

Despite the spate of recent interpretations in the field of genetics, reinforced by popular belief, I resist the suggestion that his children and his grandchildren have inherited my father's talent. I believe that every human being has a talent for acting, although certainly a whole mix of factors, individual and social, is required for our talent to achieve expression. I also resist the idea that he founded a dynasty, not simply because there were many more generations of theatre and circus people before him than have as yet descended from him. It is more because the very idea of such a dynasty puts my mother's family quite wrongly in a subordinate role. More still because it ignores or puts in the shade the many who were not actors and have no wish to act: wheelwrights, wainwrights, cordwainers (Daisy's family), farmers, chemists, clergymen, teachers (Rachel's family), pilots (Lynn's family), camera operators (mine). And most of all because acting is a profession which cannot tolerate, for long, preferment or nepotism.

Lynn began this particular journey earlier than I. She devised a play called *Shakespeare for my Father*, re-creating what Michael was to her, both as her father and as an actor. She toured the play to several countries, and in Canada last year she discovered Mr Victor Parrett – or rather he discovered her. Victor is Michael's half-brother. His story is like the magic of *A Winter's Tale*, a true and wonderful romance.

Victor's mother was an actress, Esther Mary Cooke. She was from a well-known family of circus folk, but she went on the stage and took the name Ettie Carlisle. Victor's father, as he thought, was the actor Henry Parrett, whose stage-name was Clayton.

Ettie died when Victor was sixteen, and the short remainder of his upbringing was in the care of a godmother. When Victor was twenty-one he was told that he had come into a bequest, and to claim his inheritance he had to present his birth certificate. Then began the search which led him to Somerset House and to the discovery of his real father, George Ellsworthy 'Roy' Redgrave.

How had this come to pass? Roy's first marriage, some years before he met Daisy, was to an actress called Ellen Maude Pratt, who sensibly changed her name to Judith Kyrle. By her he had four children, and might have had more if he had not met and fallen in love with Ettie Carlisle. He tried to divorce Judith for Ettie, but Ettie recoiled from the shame of being named as the third party and despite her love for Roy she knew she must leave him. She found a job in a company which was touring to South Africa, and there she married the company's leading man, Henry Parrett.

Roy must have been very much in love with Ettie because he too managed to join a touring company bound for South Africa, and there he caught up with her and wooed her all over again. Ettie left Parrett and went with Roy to Australia. She was seven months pregnant when they returned to England in 1907. And now appears the final skein of complication in an already tangled web. Roy met Daisy, in Brighton, in a play called *Their Wedding Day*. He was not the first actor to begin a new affair before the old one was finished and try to keep both going in parallel, and he might have succeeded if Daisy also had not become pregnant.

As Daisy began to apply all the pressure she knew, so pressure from Ettie, who had given birth to Roy's son, was growing. Her husband, Henry Parrett, was about to divorce her, naming Roy as co-respondent.

I would not like to have been in Roy's shoes at such a moment, on the receiving end of Daisy's wrath when she heard that he wanted to renounce his promise to marry her. However she expressed it, it was most effective, because Roy repented his change of heart and found the quickest way to marry Daisy, in Dundee, where thanks to a recent revision of marriage laws in Scotland mariners, travellers and itinerant folk such as actors were no longer required to produce documents. Just as well, because they would have revealed the fact that Roy was still married to his first wife, Judith Kyrle.

Ettie gave birth to Victor soon after. Like Michael he never knew his father. But having learned whose son he was he followed Michael's fortunes from afar and almost three-quarters of a century later they met in Vancouver. It was 1977, towards the end of my father's three-year tour of *Shakespeare's People*.

For some reason he never told us children of their meeting. Perhaps it amused him to save it up, as a secret, to be revealed at the right moment. More likely he just forgot to tell us, or thought he had done so. The first chapter of his autobiography was written long before the others and well before he learned of Victor's existence, and he must have put that meeting in Vancouver to the back of his mind by the time he and I began work on the rest of his book.

I am immensely happy that Lynn and Victor found each other. When I rang him a few days ago in Canada to introduce myself Victor said, 'Well, blow me down, Corin, what brings you on the line?'

What indeed? Nothing but our common pursuit of the continuity which binds us together in generations, the best of all possible balm for the sorrow of parting. My only wish is that my sons could have known Michael a little longer, and that he could have seen my daughter Jemma with his great-grandson Gabriel. He lives on in them, and in each one of them, in Harvey, Arden, Luke, Jemma and Gabriel, I catch him now and then looking at me.

Chronology
and
Performances and Productions

Chronology

1908, 20 March	Born Bristol, England
1921–6	Clifton College, Bristol
1922, 25 May	Father Roy Redgrave died Sydney, Australia
1927–31	Magdalene College, Cambridge BA, MA (Hons), Modern Languages
1931–4	Taught modern languages at Cranleigh School
1934	Joined Liverpool Repertory Company
1935, 18 July	Married Rachel Kempson
1936	Joined Tyrone Guthrie's company at Old Vic
1937, 30 January	Daughter Vanessa born
1937–8	At Queen's Theatre with John Gielgud's company
1939, 16 July	Son Corin born
1940, autumn	Signed People's Convention petition
1941, February	Broadcasting ban imposed by BBC
1941, 30 June	Entered Royal Navy
1943, 8 March	Daughter Lynn born
1946	Family moved to Bedford House, Chiswick

Chronology

1947	In Hollywood
1947, 18 March	Stepfather J. P. Anderson (Andy) died
1951	Season at Stratford-upon-Avon
1953	Season at Stratford-upon-Avon
1953	*An Actor's Ways and Means* published
1958	Season at Stratford-upon-Avon
1958	Mother Margaret (Daisy) Scudamore died
1958	*Mask or Face* published
1958–9	On tour with Shakespeare Memorial Company in Moscow and Leningrad
1959	Knighted
1959, August	First performance of *The Aspern Papers*, adapted by MR from Henry James, Queen's Theatre, London
1959	*The Mountebank's Tale* published
1962	At Chichester Festival Theatre in *Uncle Vanya*
1963	At Chichester Festival Theatre in *Uncle Vanya*
1963	At National Theatre at the Old Vic, London
1965	At Yvonne Arnaud Theatre, Guildford (directed and starred in opening season)
1973–8	*The Hollow Crown* and *Shakespeare's People* (international tours)
1979, 22 October	*Close of Play* directed by Harold Pinter, last appearance on London stage at National Theatre
1983	Autobiography *In My Mind's Eye* published
1985, 21 March	Died at nursing home in Denham

Performances and Productions

❧

Films are listed by their general release date
Plays produced/directed by Michael Redgrave are asterisked

AMATEUR AND SEMI-AMATEUR

DATE		CHARACTER	PLAY OR FILM AND AUTHOR, etc.	THEATRE
1921	July	Walked on	Henry IV, Part 2 (Shakespeare)	Memorial Theatre, Stratford-upon-Avon
1922	June	Second Niece	The Critic (Sheridan)	Clifton College
	December	She	A Pair of Lunatics	
		Barbara	The Private Detective (J. A. O. Muirhead)	
1923	June	Lady Mary	The Admirable Crichton (Barrie)	
	December	Cosmo Lennox	The Refugee (J. A. O. Muirhead)	
1924	June	Mrs Hardcastle	She Stoops to Conquer (Goldsmith)	
	December	Clarence	Richard III (Shakespeare)	
1925	June	Lady Macbeth	Macbeth (Shakespeare)	
	December	Reginald	Pigs in Straw (M. Redgrave)	
1926	June	The Young Man	The Bathroom Door (Gertrude Jennings)	Orthopaedic Hospital
		The Old Man	The Maker of Dreams (Harold Chapin)	
		Captain Absolute	The Rivals (Sheridan)	Clifton College

160

DATE		CHARACTER	PLAY OR FILM AND AUTHOR, etc.	THEATRE
1928	August	The Young Man	The Bathroom Door (Gertrude Jennings)	Duke of York's Camp
	October	The Cook	The Taming of the Shrew (Shakespeare)	Apollo
	June	Florindo	The Servant of Two Masters (Goldoni)	Amateur Dramatic Club, Cambridge
1929	November	The Soldier	The Soldier's Tale (Ramuz–Stravinsky)	
		The Lover	A Lover's Complaint (Shakespeare)	
	March	Edgar	King Lear (Shakespeare)	
	November	Mr Voysey	The Voysey Inheritance (Harley Granville-Barker)	
	December	Second Brother	Comus (Milton)	King's College, Cambridge, and 46 Gordon Square, London
1930	February	Rumour and Prince Hal	Henry IV, Part 2 (Shakespeare)	ADC, Cambridge
	March	Mr Pepys	The Battle of the Book (Redgrave–Turner)*	
	December	The Lover	A Lover's Complaint (Shakespeare)	Arts, London
		Second Brother	Comus (Milton)	
1931	June	Captain Brassbound	Captain Brassbound's Conversion (Shaw)	ADC, Cambridge
1932	June	Hymen	As You Like It (Shakespeare)*	Cranleigh School
	November	Ralph Rackstraw	HMS Pinafore (Gilbert–Sullivan)*	
1933	March	Samson	Samson Agonistes (Milton)*	
	June	Hamlet	Hamlet (Shakespeare)*	
	October	John Worthing	The Importance of Being Earnest (Oscar Wilde)	Guildford Rep. Co.
	November	Menelaus	The Trojan Women (Euripides)	
		Prospero	The Tempest (Shakespeare)	
1934	February	Clive Champion Cheney	The Circle (W. S. Maugham)	Cranleigh School
	March	Young Marlow	She Stoops to Conquer (Goldsmith)	Guildford Rep. Cp.
	June	Lear	King Lear (Shakespeare)*	Cranleigh School
	July	Mr Browning	The Barretts of Wimpole Street (Rudolph Besier)	Guildford Rep. Co.

PROFESSIONAL

DATE		CHARACTER	PLAY OR FILM AND AUTHOR, etc.	THEATRE
1934	August	Roy Darwin	Counsellor at Law (Elmer Rice)	Liverpool Playhouse
	September	Charles Hubbard	The Distaff Side (John Van Druten)	Liverpool Playhouse
	October	Dr Purley	A Sleeping Clergyman (James Bridie)	
		The Man	The Perfect Plot (Aubrey Ensor)	
	November	Mr Bolton	Sheppey (W. S. Maugham)	
	December	Ernest Hubbard	Heaven on Earth (Philip Johnson)	
1935	January	Melchior Feydak	Biography (S. N. Behrman)	
	February	Gaston	Villa for Sale (Sacha Guitry)	
	March	Sir Mark Loddon	Libel (Edward Wooll)	
		Richard Newton Clare	Flowers of the Forest (John Van Druten)	
	April	Horatio	Hamlet (Shakespeare)	
	May	Bill Clarke	Too Young to Marry (Martin Flavin)	
		Oliver Maitland	The Matriarch (G. B. Stern)	
	June	Sir Mark Loddon	Libel (Edward Wooll)	Winter Gardens, New Brighton
		Charles McFadden	Counsellor at Law (Elmer Rice)	
	July	Bill Clarke	Too Young to Marry (Martin Flavin)	Liverpool Playhouse
	August	Randolph Warrender	Youth at the Helm (Hubert Griffith)	
	September	Richard Barnet	Barnet's Folly (Jan Stewer)	
	October	Robert Murrison	Cornelius (J. B. Priestley)	
		Richard Brinsley Sheridan	Miss Linley of Bath (Mary D. Sheridan)	
	November	Max	The Copy (Helge Krog)	
		Trino	A Hundred Years Old (Quintero Brothers)	
	December	Gilbert Raymond	The Wind and the Rain (Merton Hodge)	
		BBC Official	Circus Boy (Michael Redgrave)	
1936	February	Rev. Ernest Dunwoody	Boyd's Shop (St John Ervine)	
	March	A Radio Announcer	And So To War (Joe Corrie)	
	April	Richard II	Richard of Bordeaux (Gordon Daviot)	
		Richard Burdon	Storm in a Teacup (James Bridie)	

162

DATE	CHARACTER	PLAY OR FILM AND AUTHOR, etc.	THEATRE
May	Tom Lambert	*Painted Sparrows* (Guy Paxton and Edward V. Hoile)	
June	Malvolio	*Twelfth Night* (Shakespeare)	
September	Ferdinand, King of Navarre	*Love's Labour's Lost* (Shakespeare)	Old Vic
October	Mr Horner	*The Country Wife* (Wycherley)	
November	Orlando	*As You Like It* (Shakespeare)	
December	Warbeck	*The Witch of Edmonton* (Dekker)	
1937 January	Laertes	*Hamlet* (Shakespeare)	
February	Orlando	*As You Like It* (Shakespeare)	New
March	Anderson	*The Bat* (Mary Roberts Rinehart and Avery Hopwood)	Embassy
April	Iachimo	Scene from *Cymbeline* (Shakespeare)	Old Vic
	Chorus	*Henry V* (Shakespeare)	
May	Christopher Drew	*A Ship Comes Home* (Daisy Fisher)	St Martin's
June	Larry Starr	*Three Set Out* (Philip Leaver)	Embassy
September	Bolingbroke	*Richard II* (Shakespeare)	Queen's
November	Charles Surface	*The School for Scandal* (Sheridan)	Queen's
1938 January	Baron Tusenbach	*The Three Sisters* (Chekhov)	
April	Chorus	*Henry V* (Shakespeare)	Old Vic
July	Orlando	Scenes from *As You Like It* (Shakespeare)	The Barn, Smallhythe
October	Alexei Turbin	*The White Guard* (Michael Bulgakov, adapted by Rodney Ackland)	Phoenix
December	Sir Andrew Aguecheek	*Twelfth Night* (Shakespeare)	Phoenix
1939 January	Gilbert	*The Lady Vanishes* (dir. Alfred Hitchcock)	FILM
March	Lord Harry Monchensey	*The Family Reunion* (T. S. Eliot)	Westminster
April	Alan Mackenzie	*Stolen Life* (dir. Paul Czinner)	FILM
May	Nicholas Brooke	*Climbing High* (dir. Carol Reed)	FILM
October	Henry Dewlip	*Springtime for Henry* (Benn W. Levy)	Provincial tour

DATE	CHARACTER	PLAY OR FILM AND AUTHOR, etc.	THEATRE
1940			
February	David Fenwick	The Stars Look Down (dir. Carol Reed)	FILM
March	Captain Macheath	The Beggar's Opera (John Gay)	Haymarket
	Romeo	Scene from Romeo and Juliet (Shakespeare)	Palace
June	Peter	A Window in London (dir. Herbert Mason)	FILM
	Charleston	Thunder Rock (Robert Ardrey)	Neighbourhood
July	Charleston	Thunder Rock (Robert Ardrey)	Globe
1941			
June	Kipps	Kipps (dir. Carol Reed)	FILM
September	Charles MacIver	Atlantic Ferry (dir. Walter Forde)	FILM
	Stanley Smith	Jeannie (dir. Harold French)	FILM
1942			
March	The Russian	The Big Blockade (dir. Charles Frend)	FILM
July		Lifeline (Norman Armstrong)*	Duchess
October	Gribaud	The Duke in Darkness (Patrick Hamilton)	St James's
1943			
February	Charleston	Thunder Rock (dir. Roy Boulting)	FILM
	Rakitin	A Month in the Country (Turgenev)	St James's
June	Lafont	Parisienne (Henry Becque, adapted by Ashley Dukes)	St James's
August		Blow Your Own Trumpet (Peter Ustinov)*	Playhouse
September		The Wingless Victory (Maxwell Anderson)*	Phoenix
1944			
March	Harry	Uncle Harry (Thomas Job)*	Garrick
1945			
June	The Colonel	Jacobowsky and the Colonel (Franz Werfel and S. N. Behrman)*	Piccadilly
July	Flight Lieut. Archdale Maxwell Frere	The Way to the Stars (dir. Anthony Asquith)	FILM
October		Dead of Night (Sequence dir. Alberto Cavalcanti)	FILM
1946			
April	Karel Hasek	The Captive Heart (dir. Basil Dearden)	FILM
July	Michael Wentworth	The Years Between (dir. Compton Bennett)	FILM
1947			
May	Carlyon	The Man Within (dir. Bernard Knowles)	FILM
November	Hamer Radshaw	Fame is the Spur (dir. Roy Boulting)	FILM
December	Macbeth	Macbeth (Shakespeare)	Aldwych

DATE	CHARACTER	PLAY OR FILM AND AUTHOR, etc.	THEATRE
1948 March	Macbeth	Macbeth (Shakespeare)	National, New York
November	The Captain	The Father (Strindberg)	Embassy
December	Mark Lamphere	Secret Beyond the Door (dir. Fritz Lang)	FILM
1949 January	The Captain	The Father (Strindberg)	Duchess
April	Etienne	A Woman in Love (M. Redgrave and Diana Gould, from G. de Porto-Riche)*	Embassy
October	Berowne	Love's Labour's Lost (Shakespeare)	New
	Young Marlow	She Stoops to Conquer (Shakespeare)	New
1950 November	Rakitin	A Month in the Country (Turgenev)	New
February	Hamlet	Hamlet (Shakespeare)	Kronborg Castle
June	Hamlet	Hamlet	Drury Lane
November	Filmer Jesson	Scene from His House in Order (Pinero)	Holland
December		Solo performances of Shakespeare	Stratford-upon-Avon
1951 March	Richard II	Richard II (Shakespeare)	FILM
April	Hotspur	Henry IV, Part 1 (Shakespeare)	Stratford-upon-Avon
	Andrew Crocker-Harris	The Browning Version (dir. Anthony Asquith)	Holland Festival
May		Henry IV, Part 2 (Shakespeare)*	Stratford-upon-Avon
June	Prospero	The Tempest (Shakespeare)	St James's
July		Solo performances of Shakespeare	FILM
July	Chorus	Henry V (Shakespeare)	FILM
1952 April	Mr Lege	The Magic Box (dir. John Boulting)	Stratford-upon-Avon
July	Frank Elgin	Winter Journey (Clifford Odets)	Prince's
	John Worthing	The Importance of Being Earnest (dir. Anthony Asquith)	
July	Orin Mannon	Mourning Becomes Electra (dir. Dudley Nichols; released New York 1947)	
1953 March	Shylock	The Merchant of Venice (Shakespeare)	
April	Antony	Antony and Cleopatra (Shakespeare)	
July	Lear	King Lear (Shakespeare)	
November	Antony	Antony and Cleopatra (Shakespeare)	

DATE		CHARACTER	PLAY OR FILM AND AUTHOR, etc.	THEATRE
1954	January	Antony	Antony and Cleopatra (Shakespeare)	The Hague, Amsterdam, Antwerp, Brussels and Paris
	September	Maître Déliot	The Green Scarf (dir. George More O'Ferrall)	FILM
1955	January	Air Commodore Waltby	The Sea Shall Not Have Them (dir. Lewis Gilbert)	FILM
		Colonel Eisenstein	Oh, Rosalinda! (dir. Michael Powell and Emeric Pressburger)	FILM
	April	The Air Marshal	The Night My Number Came Up (dir. Leslie Norman)	FILM
	June	Barnes Wallis	The Dam Busters (dir. Michael Anderson)	FILM
		Hector	Tiger at the Gates (Jean Giraudoux, trans. Christopher Fry)	Apollo
	October	Hector	Tiger at the Gates	Plymouth, New York
	November	Trebitsch	Confidential Report (dir. Orson Welles)	FILM
	December	Shylock	Tubal scene in The Merchant of Venice (Shakespeare)	Waldorf-Astoria
1956	March	O'Connor	1984 (dir. Michael Anderson)	FILM
	April		A Month in the Country (Turgenev)*	Phoenix, New York
	November	The Regent	The Sleeping Prince (Terence Rattigan)	Coronet, New York
1957	January	Ruggles	Ruggles of Red Gap	NBC TV
	March	David Graham	Time Without Pity (dir. Joseph Losey)	FILM
	June	General Medworth	The Happy Road (dir. Gene Kelly)	FILM
	September	Narrator	Vanishing Cornwall (Christian Browning)	FILM
1958	January	Philip Lester	A Touch of the Sun (N. C. Hunter)	Saville
	March	Fowler	The Quiet American (dir. Joseph L. Mankiewicz)	FILM
	June	Hamlet	Hamlet (Shakespeare) (dir. Glen Byam Shaw)	Stratford-upon-Avon
		Percy	Law and Disorder (dir. Charles Crichton)	FILM
	August	Benedick	Much Ado About Nothing (Shakespeare)	Stratford-upon-Avon
	October	Narrator	The Immortal Land (dir. Basil Wright)	FILM
	November	Hamlet	Hamlet (Shakespeare)	Palace of Culture, Leningrad and Moscow Art Theatre,

DATE		CHARACTER	PLAY OR FILM AND AUTHOR, etc.	THEATRE
1959	August	Sir Arthur Benson Gray	Behind the Mask (dir. Brian Desmond Hurst)	FILM
		HJ	The Aspern Papers (Henry James: adapted by MR)*	Queen's
	May	Michael Collins	Shake Hands with the Devil (dir. Michael Anderson)	FILM
	December	Mr Nyland	The Wreck of the Mary Deare (dir. Michael Anderson)	FILM
1960	April	Jack Dean	Solo performances of Shakespeare	Ordry, Budapest
	August		The Tiger and the Horse (Robert Bolt)	Queen's
1961	June		Solo performances of Shakespeare and Hans Andersen	Bath Festival
	August	Sir Matthew Carr	No, My Darling Daughter (dir. Betty Box and Ralph Thomas)	FILM
	November	The Uncle	The Innocents (dir. Jack Clayton)	FILM
1962	July	Victor Rhodes	The Complaisant Lover (Graham Greene)	Ethel Barrymore, New York
	September	Vanya	Uncle Vanya (Chekhov)	Chichester Festival
		Governor	The Loneliness of the Long-Distance Runner (dir. Tony Richardson)	FILM
1963	November	Lancelot Dodd	Out of Bounds (Arthur Watkyn)	Wyndham's
	December	Tesman	Hedda Gabler (Ibsen)	BBC TV
	May	General Cavendish	Return to the Regiment (dir. John Moxey)	ITV
	July	Vanya	Uncle Vanya (Chekhov)	Chichester Festival
	October	Claudius	Hamlet (Shakespeare)	Old Vic (National Theatre)
	November	Vanya	Uncle Vanya (Chekhov)	
1964	January	Henry Hobson	Hobson's Choice (Harold Brighouse)	
	April	Narrator	The Great War (John Terraine and Corelli Barnett)	BBC TV
1965	June	Solness	The Master Builder (Ibsen)	Old Vic (National Theatre)
	November	Reader	Tribute to President Kennedy	ABC TV
	March	W. B. Yeats	Young Cassidy (dir. Jack Cardiff)	FILM

DATE	CHARACTER	PLAY OR FILM AND AUTHOR, etc.	THEATRE
May	Rakitin	A Month in the Country (Turgenev)	Yvonne Arnaud, Guildford
June	Samson	Samson Agonistes (Milton)	
	Uncle	The Heroes of Telemark (dir. Anthony Mann)	FILM
September	The MO	The Hill (dir. Sidney Lumet)	FILM
1966 June	Rakitin	A Month in the Country (Turgenev)	Cambridge, London
October		Werther (Massenet)*	Glyndebourne Opera
December	Narrator	The Lost Peace (John Terraine)	BBC TV
	The Blue Caterpillar	Alice in Wonderland (Lewis Carroll)	BBC TV
1967 June		La Bohème (Puccini)*	Glyndebourne Opera
November	Commentary	October Revolution (Fred Nossif)	BBC Radio
December	Charles Dickens	Mr Dickens of London (Barry Morse)	ABC TV
1968 January	Monsieur Barnett	Monsieur Barnett (Jean Anouilh)	BBC TV
	Harris	Assignment K (dir. Val Guest)	FILM
May	Reading from The Huntingdonshire Cabmen	World of Beachcomber	BBC TV
	Prospero	The Tempest (Shakespeare)	BBC TV
November	The Ghost	The Canterville Ghost	ABC TV
1969 April	Grandfather	Heidi	NBC TV
	General Wilson	Oh, What A Lovely War (dir. Richard Attenborough)	FILM
September	Air Vice-Marshal Evill	Battle of Britain (dir. Guy Hamilton)	FILM
November	The Headmaster	Goodbye, Mr Chips (dir. Herbert Ross)	FILM
1970 March	Mr Peggotty	David Copperfield (dir. Delbert Mann)	FILM
August	The MP	Goodbye Gemini (dir. Alan Gibson)	FILM
1971 April	The Commander	Hell scene from Man and Superman (G. B. Shaw)	BBC TV
April	Polonius	Hamlet (Shakespeare)	TV, USA; BBC TV, UK
May	James Wallraven	Connecting Rooms (dir. Franklin Gollings)	FILM
July	Mr Jaraby	The Old Boys (William Trevor)	Mermaid Theatre, London
August	Father	A Voyage Round My Father (John Mortimer)	Haymarket

DATE		CHARACTER	PLAY OR FILM AND AUTHOR, etc.	THEATRE
1972	April	Grand Duke	Nicholas and Alexandra (dir. Franklin Shaffner)	FILM
	September	John	A Voyage Round My Father (John Mortimer)	Tour of Canada and Australia
	December	Erik Fritsch	The Pump (James Cameron)	BBC Radio
			The Last Target (dir. George Spenton-Foster)	FILM
			Reading of Child's Christmas in Wales for the National Theatre of the Deaf	CBS
1973	August		Reading The Hollow Crown (Shakespeare)	Central City, Denver, and Opera House, Washington
1974			Reading The Hollow Crown (Shakespeare) and Pleasure and Repentance (programme of poetry, prose and songs)	USA tour
1975	January		Reading The Hollow Crown (Shakespeare) and Pleasure and Repentance (poetry, prose and songs)	World tour
1976	August		Reading Shakespeare's People (Shakespeare)	South Africa
	October		Reading Shakespeare's People (Shakespeare)	Tour of South America and Canada
	November		Reading The Wheel of Fire (Shakespeare)	Theatre Royal, Windsor, and English tour
1977	March		Reading Shakespeare's People (Shakespeare)	Tour of Denmark, Canada, New Zealand and USA
1978	January		Reading Shakespeare's People (Shakespeare)	Bermuda Festival
	April		Reading from Hans Andersen	Palaeets Lesser Hall, Copenhagen
1979	September		Reading Shakespeare's People (Shakespeare)	Arts Theatre, Cambridge
	May	Jasper	Close of Play (Simon Gray) (dir. by Harold Pinter)	National Theatre, London
	October		Close of Play (Simon Gray)	Royal, Bath
			Close of Play (Simon Gray)	Olympia, Dublin
1982			Scene from King Lear (Shakespeare)	Roundhouse

Index

Index

Index